Year 1597 by *GULIELMUS HAIWA*

W9-BLV-158

92
SKAIFE

Skaife, Christopher,
1965-

The Ravenmaster.

THE RAVENMASTER

The Ravenmaster

MY LIFE WITH THE RAVENS
AT THE TOWER OF LONDON

Christopher Skaife

YEOMAN WARDER OF HER MAJESTY'S
ROYAL PALACE AND FORTRESS
THE TOWER OF LONDON

FARRAR, STRAUS AND GIROUX   NEW YORK

Farrar, Straus and Giroux
175 Varick Street, New York 10014

Library of Congress Cataloging-in-Publication Data
Names: Skaife, Christopher, 1965– author.
Title: The Ravenmaster : my life with the ravens at the Tower of London /
  Ravenmaster Christopher Skaife, Yeoman Warder of Her Majesty's
  Royal Palace and Fortress the Tower of London.
Description: First edition. | New York : Farrar, Straus and Giroux, 2018. |
  Includes index.
Identifiers: LCCN 2018016402 | ISBN 9780374113346 (hardcover)
Subjects: LCSH: Skaife, Christopher, 1965– | Yeomen Warders—Biography. |
  Tower of London (London, England) | Ravens—England.
Classification: LCC DA687.T7 S595 2018 | DDC 942.1/5 [B] —dc23
LC record available at https://lccn.loc.gov/2018016402

Designed by Jonathan D. Lippincott

www.fsgbooks.com
www.twitter.com/fsgbooks • www.facebook.com/fsgbooks

1   3   5   7   9   10   8   6   4   2

*To the ravens of Her Majesty's Royal Palace
and Fortress the Tower of London
And to the memory of Martin Harris*

CONTENTS

THE RAVENMASTER

1

SILHOUETTE

It's 0530. Autumn. First light over London. I'm up and out of bed before the alarm. I get dressed in the dark and head straight out the door. No time even for a cup of tea. There's always that niggling concern that something might have gone wrong overnight. And if things go wrong, things can go badly wrong.

I can already hear the lorries and the white vans and the early morning commuters coming into town. Tower Bridge Road, Fenchurch Street, London Bridge. There's that hum—the sound of the city awakening.

I hurry up the stone spiral staircase by the Flint Tower, the London skyline bright with lights and winking behind me. I see the old Port of London Authority Building, which is now home to a fancy hotel, but was once responsible for the comings and goings of ships all the way up and down the Thames. Behind that stand the Cheesegrater and the Walkie-Talkie and the Gherkin, the big new skyscrapers with their funny little nicknames.

Past the Chapel and the Waterloo Barracks and out onto Tower Green and there's that proper morning smell of London, that mixture of exhaust fumes, the Thames, fresh ground coffee, and the beautiful sweet incongruous smell of fresh-cut grass on Tower Green. Tower Bridge is hunched up ahead, with HMS *Belfast* reliably anchored on the River to the south.

There's no one around in the Tower, just me and the shadows of a thousand years of history.

I call out and at first there's nothing but silence. I call out again. There's always that moment of fear as I scan the skyline. But then I see her: perched on one of the rooftops of the Tower buildings, a silhouette against the blue-gray dawn.

"Good morning," I say.

And a good morning it is.

The ravens are at home in the Tower.

I can breathe easy again—the kingdom is safe for another day.

RAVENMASTER

I have what is often described as the oddest job in Britain.

Odd? Maybe.

The best? Definitely.

My name is Chris Skaife and I am the Ravenmaster at the Tower of London.

My official title is Yeoman Warder Christopher Skaife, of Her Majesty's Royal Palace and Fortress the Tower of London, and member of the Sovereign's Body Guard of the Yeoman Guard Extraordinary, which is generally believed to be the oldest formed "Body of Men" in the world still in existence, dating back to the reign of King Henry VII sometime after the Battle of Bosworth Field in 1485. All of us Yeoman Warders are former servicemen and -women, with at least twenty-two years of unblemished service. We are the ceremonial guardians of the Tower of London. In principle we're responsible for looking after any prisoners at the Tower and safeguarding the Crown Jewels. In practice, we act as tour guides and as custodians of the rituals of the Tower. We live right here, in the Tower. They say that every man's home is his castle: for us, it's literally the case.

How can I begin to explain the Tower to you? It was built as a fortress and a royal palace, but it's also been a prison, an arsenal, and the site of the Royal Mint and the Royal Armoury. One of the great early English historians, John Stow—who grew up about half a mile from the Tower—summed it up best in his *Survey of London*, published in 1598: "This Tower is a citadel to defend or command the city; a royal palace for assemblies or treaties; a prison of state for the most dangerous offenders; the only place of coinage for all England at this time; the armoury for warlike provision; the treasury of the ornaments and jewels of the crown; and general conserver of the most records of the king's courts of justice at Westminster." That just about covers it. These days we welcome around three million visitors every year.

•

There are plenty of famous places for tourists and locals to visit in London. There's Westminster Abbey, as well as the Houses of Parliament, Buckingham Palace, Kensington Palace, Kew Gardens, Hampton Court Palace, the British Museum, the Imperial War Museums, the Victoria and Albert, the Science Museum, the Natural History Museum. The list goes on and on. If you're the sort of person who wants to see a nice baroque interior, then off you can go to a Hawksmoor church, or if you fancy a nice bit of postwar Brutalism, there's the Royal Festival Hall. If you're looking for a good view, you can go to Hampstead Heath or Primrose Hill, or up to the top of the Shard. You've got your theaters and your concert halls and your restaurants and cafés. But in my opinion— my humble opinion—the Tower remains without a doubt one of London's great attractions.

Why? Well, there's the obvious fact that we're one of the *first* attractions. When William the Conqueror defeated King Harold at the Battle of Hastings back in 1066 he decided he needed a sign of his triumph, a monument to his great power and strength, and so sometime around the late 1070s work began on the White Tower, the biggest and boldest building ever undertaken in England. The Tower was intended as a symbol of power and remains so today: in my opinion, the finest example of statement architecture in the country. London may be forever reinventing itself, but the Tower remains. Much of the old city was destroyed in the Great Fire of 1666. Since then, Newgate Prison has gone. Old London Bridge has gone. The great warehouses around St. Katharine Docks have gone. Even during my time at the Tower, London has been transformed: the Shard, the Gherkin, the Walkie-Talkie; Crossrail; the Docklands Light Railway; the gentrification of the East End. Yet right in the middle of it all we still have the Tower. It has seen it all, done it all, been part of it all. It has incredible architecture. Pageantry. A bloody history of murder and torture. And—of course—it has the ravens.

We currently have seven ravens at the Tower. As the Ravenmaster I'm the person responsible for their safety, security, and welfare. I look after the ravens—and the ravens look after us. Without the ravens, so the legend goes, the Tower itself will crumble into dust and great harm will befall the kingdom.

This book will attempt to answer some of the most common questions I get asked about the Tower ravens. Why are there ravens at the Tower in the first place? Where do our myths and superstitions about the birds come from? How do I care for them? What do I feed them? Who gets to name them? What happens to them when they die? How and why do they stay at the Tower?

What this book is not—I should state clearly at the outset—is a scientific study. I am not a scientist, though over the years I've been fortunate to meet with and assist the many scientists who have come and studied our birds and who have written about them in academic journals and reports. Despite my many years of experience looking after the ravens, I don't have any official bird-related credentials or qualifications. I am not a professional ornithologist. I'm really just an average guy with a greater-than-average amount of luck who has been fortunate enough to have spent a large part of my life with some of the most famous birds in the world as they go about their daily business. This book is about my life and work with the Tower ravens, and what it takes to be the Ravenmaster.

·

I was born and brought up in Dover, in the county of Kent, in the southeast of England. My earliest memory is when I was barely a toddler, climbing out onto the ledge of our living room window. I was right there, ready to go, before I was pulled back in. An early bid for freedom. There was another time, a few years later, when I climbed a big old gnarly tree until I was positioned right above our neighbor's greenhouse—and then I jumped. I wanted to see what would happen. What happened was that I went straight through the glass. I've still got the scars to show for it.

By the time I was about fifteen I was bunking off school and going to the woods or up to the local hills as part of a little gang of kids. We kept ourselves busy by lighting fires, drinking cider, stealing stuff, and generally mucking around. We had our sheath knives to build dens and make arrows and we would break into old storerooms and garages to see what was there—just getting up to mischief. We'd buy fireworks and put bangers in car exhausts or fire them out of old plumbing pipes. We stole a couple of motorbikes and took them up to the hills to go scrambling. We tried to steal a Ford Anglia, but it had a dead battery and we were swiftly caught by the police. I remember getting a thick ear for that.

I wasn't a bad kid, but I wasn't the best.

This was 1981. If you switched on the TV it was all the Yorkshire Ripper this, and the Hunger Strikers that, and the Brixton and the Toxteth riots, and the National Front were marching, and Enoch Powell was sounding off about a race war, and AIDS was becoming a global crisis, and unemployment figures were skyrocketing. Thatcher was in power. The IRA were bombing and killing soldiers and civilians. It was what you might call a bit of a difficult period in British history.

And there we were, at the beginning of a new decade, boys and girls about to leave school and ready for some adventures of our own.

My parents were getting concerned. I was drinking, smoking, going to parties, sneaking out to sleep up in the hills, getting into fights with other gangs. What was to be done with me?

And then one day an Army careers advisor visited the school. It happened to be one of the days I was actually attending classes.

Like a lot of kids back then I had spent a lot of my childhood reenacting the Second World War, playing with toy soldiers, staging fights and battles with my mates, Allies versus the Nazis, all that sort of thing, reading the old 1970s war comics, *The Victor* and *Warlord* and *Battle*. There was *Dad's Army* on TV, of course, as well as *Kojak* and *The Six Million Dollar Man*, and *Kung Fu* and *Planet of the Apes*—it was all goodies and baddies and tough guys and fighting. So, when the Army careers advisor gave us his talk and handed out his leaflets about joining the army—a life full of adventure, a life of goodies and baddies and tough guys and fighting—I thought it seemed like a pretty good idea. I took the leaflets home and talked to my parents, who probably thought, well, if it's not that, he's going to end up in jail.

I went with Mum to the old Army Careers Information Office in Dover, which was just a little red brick hut really, tucked away at the base of the cliffs, by the eastern dock and the ferry terminal, and there was this portly old recruiting sergeant sitting in there and you could see he was bored out of his mind, and all you had to do was a basic literacy and numeracy test and then sign on the dotted line and take the Queen's shilling and you were in, more or less. So I did.

It was the best decision I ever made.

Off I went to Deepcut Barracks to do a fitness test, interviews, a general knowledge test. I was asked if I wanted to learn a trade because my test results were that good. I was a "messer," as we say in the U.K., but I wasn't stupid. I could have trained as an engineer, or even a veterinary nurse. I could have learned a proper trade, but by that time the Falklands War had started and I just wanted to learn to fire a gun and be a soldier and get on with it. So I chose to go in as a good old-fashioned regular soldier. I left school, my parents took me to Dover Priory train station, I waved goodbye to them, and I joined the army as a boy soldier, the Junior Infantry Battalion at Bassingbourn, on June 18, 1982, which as it turned out was just a few days after British forces had recaptured Stanley from the Argentinians, and the Falklands War was over. I was sixteen and a half. That was the beginning of almost twenty-five years in the military—a full-service career which took me all over the world and eventually to the Tower of London and into the lives of my friends, the ravens.

I'm very lucky to have had two careers: as a soldier and now as a Yeoman Warder. As a soldier I saw the best and worst of what humans are capable of. As the Ravenmaster I've been granted a privileged insight into the life and behavior of some of the world's most extraordinary nonhuman creatures. One of the things I've learned from the ravens is that they're surprisingly like us: they are versatile, adaptable, omnivorous; they are capable of great cruelty and great kindness; and on the whole they manage to get along with one another. In learning about the ravens, I have discovered a lot about what it means to be a human: I've learned to listen, to observe, and to be still. The ravens have been my teachers and I have been their pupil.

•

There's a photograph of me as a young boy on a school trip to London. Trafalgar Square. We'd come up from Kent on the train for the day. It was a real treat—London Town! I'm kneeling, wearing flared trousers and sporting a bowl-cut hairstyle—this was the 1970s, after all—and I am concentrating on feeding the pigeons. You can see from the photo that I am completely and utterly absorbed. You can see the expression on my face, me thinking, what are those birds about?

That fascination is with me still. My hope is that in reading this book you too will become fascinated.

THE RULES

I am, as far as I'm aware, only the sixth Ravenmaster ever to have been appointed at the Tower. Before that, caring for the ravens was part of the job of the Yeoman Quartermaster. Like a lot of our great traditions in Great Britain, the role and indeed the title of Ravenmaster is in fact a recent invention. The story goes that when Henry Johns was appointed Yeoman Quartermaster just after World War II, some of the old Yeoman Warders used to joke that he was raving mad—so keen was he on caring for the birds—and so he affectionately became known as the Raving Master instead of the Quartermaster. It wasn't until John Wilmington took over from Henry Johns in 1968 that the more sane-sounding title of Raven Master became official, and not until some years later—doubtless due to some clerical error in a back office somewhere—that the Raven Master became known as the Ravenmaster.*

---

*For a full list of Ravenmasters, see the appendix.

I lead a team of Yeoman Warders here at the Tower who assist me in caring for the birds. They are known as the Ravenmaster's assistants. I call us Team Raven. Together we are responsible for looking after the ravens 365 days a year. There's never a day when there's not a Yeoman Warder on duty caring for the ravens. They are possibly the most cared for—and certainly the best-loved—birds in the world.

There are a few simple rules about caring for the Tower ravens that have been passed down to me over the years by my illustrious predecessors, and which I in turn like to pass on to my assistants. The theory goes that if you follow these rules you'll remain safe around the ravens, and they'll remain safe around you.

DO NOT hurry the ravens.
DO NOT attempt to change the pecking order.
DO NOT try to cut corners.
DO remain calm at all times.
DO allow the ravens to follow the same routine every
    day.
DO prepare for chaos if you break any of the above
    rules.

It goes without saying that I have failed to observe these rules many times—and that the job of Ravenmaster is in fact rather more challenging and complex than following a few basic rules.

As Ravenmaster you have to be able to think on your feet. Over the years I've had to deal with bird-on-bird attacks, bird-on-human attacks, human-on-bird attacks, stolen goods, snatched food, biohazard concerns, security problems, disease, death, and tragedy. On a daily basis my job involves dealing with children, tour guides, VIPs, journalists, amateur historians, professional historians, bird lovers, and all the other assorted visitors to the Tower. By my calculation, in the height of the summer, when our visitor numbers are at their peak, I am photographed about three or four hundred times a day, every day: I reckon the ravens and I have probably featured in someone's family album in every country in the world. For the love of ravens I've nearly drowned, I've very nearly fallen off tall buildings, and many's the time I've had to risk my reputation and stick my neck out to try to do what I think's best for the birds. And it's not as if they're exactly grateful. They are not my pets. They do not do tricks. They do not ride unicycles. They do not speak Latin. They don't necessarily do what I tell them to do—which can be more than a little embarrassing. There was the time one of our ravens affectionately pecked a cameraman on the back of the leg during a television interview about the Tower, for example: that caused a bit of a commotion. They do not perform on cue. The Tower ravens are big, unpredictable creatures, with a powerful bite, who roam freely about the Tower and who have the ability to fly off at any moment if they so desire.

•

So, you have been warned. You know the rules. Now it's time to meet the ravens.

ROLL CALL

As I mentioned, we currently have seven ravens at the Tower. We always have a minimum of six—as decreed, according to legend, by Charles II. These are our magnificent seven:

MUNIN

Female

Entered Tower service May 18, 1995

Age on arrival: six weeks old

Current age: twenty-two years old

Presented by Mrs. Joyce Ross

Named by Ravenmaster David Cope

Raven Munin is currently the oldest serving raven at
the Tower.*

---

*The longest-ever-serving raven at the Tower was James Crow, who entered service around 1880 and didn't pass away until 1924, making him an incredible forty-four years old. Ravens in the wild would be lucky to live into their teens or twenties. We would of course never name a raven James Crow these days—times, thank goodness, have changed.

Raven Munin—named after one of Odin's ravens in Norse mythology—has led what you might call a colorful life.

She is incredibly intelligent—she can solve scientific tests in record time. She is also tough and she is brave: she loves to get as high up around the Tower as she possibly can, which has caused me no end of problems, having to clamber up after her. She's broken her wing twice and is now permanently on medication to treat her arthritis. She's had three partners during her time with us—two of them now dead—and so is affectionately known to me and my assistants as the Black Widow.

I'll be honest: Munin and I have something of a troubled relationship. Basically, she doesn't like me. In fact, sometimes I think she actually hates me. She's certainly been giving me the runaround for years. Research suggests that ravens can recognize human faces, and I can only assume that I did something horrendous in my early days as the old Ravenmaster's assistant and Munin has never forgiven me.

If you ever visit the Tower, you can easily identify Munin because she's the bird who hops off in the opposite direction whenever she sees me! After many years of niggling, tussling, and negotiation, I would describe ours as a relationship of mutual grudging respect.

MERLIN/MERLINA

Female (but thought male for the first five years of
her life)

Entered Tower service May 2007

Age on arrival: one year old

Current age: eleven years old

Place of origin: somewhere in Wales

Presented by Anne Bird, Barry Swan Rescue center

Named by previous owner and officially still known
     in Tower records as Merlin (renamed Merlina by
     Ravenmaster Chris Skaife)

Merlina was found by the side of a road in Wales. She was adopted by a family of bird lovers who built her an aviary and looked after her until she became too difficult to handle. She is not a bird suited to a quiet suburban life. Her caretakers gave her to the Swan Rescue center in Barry, Wales, where she quickly became renowned for throwing tantrums, mimicking other birds, and randomly squawking out a primitive "Hello" and "Thank you" at passersby. After she refused to have anklets placed on her and withdrew all cooperation in her interactions with her carers, the Rescue contacted us at the Tower in desperation. And here she has been, perfectly happy, ever since.

Unlike my uneasy relationship with Munin, Merlina and I are close. Very close. Indeed—after many years—she has bonded with me and two of my assistants and is always very friendly toward us. She is *not*, however, friendly toward anybody else—including our fellow Yeoman Warders.

Over the past few years, Merlina has become quite a celebrity. She has her own dedicated followers on Twitter, Instagram, and Facebook. She receives gifts and cards and letters from well-wishers and has appeared countless times on television and in newspaper and magazine articles. She likes playing with sticks while rolling on her back, calling out to the crows to come play with her, doing forward rolls, stealing stuff from unsuspecting members of the public, playing in the snow, playing dead, drinking water out of the fountain, washing potato chips if she doesn't like the flavor, emptying the bins on the endless search for food, hunting mice, and stalking pigeons.

Merlina could fly off to a new life if she so desired, but due to the nature of our bonding, and with a bit of careful flight-feather trimming, we've managed to keep her here at the Tower. She is our most free-spirited bird: she's also my closest friend among the ravens.

In many ways, Merlina is a bit of a loner: she refuses to socialize with any of the other ravens. I think of her as the Tower Princess. If another raven goes anywhere near her, she hops along to find me to seek my protection, often bringing me little treats to share, usually rotten meat or rats' tails. Her favorite activity is to sit with me in the Bloody Tower sentry box and fall asleep while I gently stroke her feathers. Whatever you do, do *not* try this if you visit with her. Not if you value your fingers.

ERIN

Female
Entered Tower service 2006
Age on arrival: six weeks old
Current age: eleven years old

Place of origin: Yatton, Somerset
Presented by Mr. Martin Harris
Named by Ravenmaster Derrick Coyle

It's said that ravens mate for life, but in my experience Raven Erin's partnership with Raven Rocky is a rather more complex process than is often assumed by us humans. What I can say is that Erin and Rocky like to perch together, fly together, walk together, and preen together. They're a classic couple in many ways—and in this partnership, it is Erin who most definitely wears the trousers.

Erin may be one of our smallest ravens, but she is by far the noisiest. She likes nothing better first thing in the morning than crawing and cronking at the top of her voice and annoying the residents of the Tower. She's not, shall we say, a bird who is backward in coming forward. She will chat away forever, is extremely boisterous, and loves to pester the other ravens. One of her favorite games is to invade another bird's territory, pick a fight, cause all sorts of commotion, and then suddenly back off. With Erin, I often find myself having to assume the role of policeman. If she's on Tower Green, for example, squawking at Merlina, I'll intervene with a wag of my finger and tell her to move along, and then off she goes.

Erin and I are not exactly close, but we get along fine. We have a few volunteers at the Tower who like to assist with our work with the birds, and over the years Erin has befriended one or two of them, whom she graciously allows to feed her the occasional nut or biscuit.

Many of our American visitors like to point out that the

name Erin is Irish, though I like to point out in return that it is in fact a Hiberno-English derivative of the Irish word "Éirinn," meaning Ireland, and no, she's not from Ireland. She's from Somerset. The naming of the ravens can sometimes seem nonsensical—and indeed paradoxical and ironic, as is the case with Erin's partner, the wonderfully though inappropriately named Rocky.

ROCKY

Male
Entered Tower service July 2011
Age on arrival: three years old
Current age: nine years old
Place of origin: Yatton, Somerset
Presented by Mr. Martin Harris
Named by Ravenmaster Chris Skaife

Traditionally our ravens were named after the person who presented them to the Tower. Thus, Raven Edward, who was presented to the Tower around 1890 and who was named after Colonel Edward Treffry from the Honourable Artillery Company. Or one of my favorites, the legendary raven Edgar Sopper, presented in 1923 and named after Colonel Sopper. All of our ravens these days are bred outside the Tower by a small number of recognized breeders and acquired by the Tower as and when we need them, so our naming practices have had to change. We once had a Ronald Raven, for example, so named by viewers of the children's television program *Blue Peter.* We've had ravens named Cedric, Sandy, Mabel,

Pauline, and—in tribute to the character played by Tony Robinson in the TV comedy *Blackadder*—Baldrick.

Rocky is in fact named after the former Ravenmaster Rocky Stones, and not after the boxer played by Sylvester Stallone, which is probably for the best because Rocky is most definitely not a fighter. Admittedly he does have a distinctive short fat beak, which makes him look a bit like he has a broken nose and is about to land a heavy punch on you. He's big and he likes to swagger around a bit, and he does his best to protect Erin when she gets into trouble, but he's really a very shy, sweet-natured sort of a bird. In fact, he's a bit of a softy. He follows Erin around like a little puppy, is completely uninterested in me or in the public, and likes nothing more than to spend his time snuggling up to her, though how on earth he puts up with her incessant squawking I have absolutely no idea.

JUBILEE II

Male

Entered Tower Service May 2013

Age on arrival: six weeks old

Current age: four years old

Place of origin: Yatton, Somerset

Presented by Mr. Martin Harris

Named Jubilee by popular demand

Jubilee II started out life as a stand-in. In 2012, in honor of the Queen's Diamond Jubilee, the Tower authorities thought it might be a nice idea to give Her Majesty a raven as a present.

We'd keep it here on her behalf and look after it for her. Shortly after presenting the bird, I went away on holiday to the United States. Just a few hours after my arrival, I received a frantic phone call from one of my colleagues.

"Chris, there's a bit of a problem."

"What's that?"

"Two ravens have died."

"Which ravens?"

"Jubilee and Gripp."

"Died?"

"Killed."

"Foxes?"

"Foxes."

"So you're telling me I've just come all this way to the U.S. on holiday and the Queen's new raven has been killed by a fox?"

"Yep. Sorry, mate."

It was not a great start to my long-awaited holiday, but fortunately we were quickly able to acquire some replacement ravens, whom we named Jubilee II and Gripp II.

Jubilee II is currently Munin's partner. I say "currently" because when Munin dies, I might try to pair Jubilee II with Merlina. Merlina has recently started to allow Jubilee II to spend a little time with her on Tower Green, which is very unusual. Merlina, as I said, is not a bird who usually tolerates the company of other ravens. There's a bit of an age difference between Merlina and Jubilee II, but they seem to get on and I can certainly see why. Jubilee II is very much the strong silent type: well-behaved, well-groomed. Perfect boyfriend material. I think of Jubilee as a knight of the Tower.

GRIPP II

Male
Entered Tower service May 2013
Age on arrival: six weeks old
Current age: four years old
Place of origin: Yatton, Somerset
Presented by Mr. Martin Harris
Named by Ravenmaster Chris Skaife

Gripp is the opposite of Jubilee: tiny and rather frail. We assume that Gripp is male—but I rather fancy that *he* is in fact a *she*. It wouldn't be the first time that one of our male birds turned out to be female. As I mentioned, Merlina started out life as Merlin, and there have doubtless been other examples of mistaken identity during the history of the Tower ravens. The sexing of birds is notoriously difficult, even for vets, never mind for Yeoman Warders. Ravens not only lack external sexual organs, like most species of birds, but the male and female are almost identical in appearance, and there are no great differences in behavior. It's not as if the males have brighter plumage or different feather patterns, or wattles or combs or crests or leg spurs that might help you distinguish them from females. To the untrained eye, the only noticeable difference is that the male ravens tend to have a slightly longer middle toe and thicker bills, but then again, we've had female birds before with great thick bills, and measuring the difference in ravens' toes is not a hobby for the fainthearted. Handling the birds can make them extremely stressed at the best of times, so really the only way to determine Gripp's sex would be to take a feather and have it DNA tested. Since Gripp seems perfectly happy as s/he is and because we treat all the birds equally here at the Tower anyway, whatever their sex and gender, there seems little point in putting him/her through the stress. So, for the moment Gripp remains a he—a rather timid and shy he, admittedly, who requires a little bit more looking after than some of the other birds. I have a bit of a soft spot for him and don't like to see him being picked on or bullied by the others.

HARRIS

Male

Entered Tower Service May 2016

Age on arrival: six weeks old

Current age: one year old

Place of origin: Yatton, Somerset

Presented by Miss Lori Burchill

Named by Ravenmaster Assistant Shady Lane

Harris is the youngest and the biggest of our current birds. You can tell he's young—if you can get close enough—because the inside of his mouth is pink. The raven mouth turns black as the bird ages, in much the same way as our hair turns gray. Harris will be counted as a juvenile for about three years before coming into full maturity, though he's already started displaying signs of adult behavior. Just a couple of weeks ago he spent three days up on the rooftops of the Tower, checking things out, only returning to be with the other ravens because he was hungry. I fancy he's going to keep me rather busy in the years to come.

Harris is named after Martin Harris, a breeder who presented us with more than a dozen ravens during his lifetime—including most of our current birds—and who was a real character, and someone greatly loved by all of Team Raven.

Harris was in fact hatched on the very day of our old friend Martin's funeral, which I attended down in Somerset with my Deputy Ravenmaster, Shady Lane, both of us in full uniform. I can well remember driving down a few weeks later to collect the new little birdling, which was a bittersweet moment for us all, and we decided there and then to name the new bird after Martin, as a reminder of the many people who love the ravens and who have been involved in their well-being.

I hope and trust that Harris will have a long and happy life ahead of him.

5

BIRD LIFE

Having met the ravens, you'll probably be wanting to get a sense of their living arrangements.

It's perhaps easiest to visualize where we all live at the Tower if you imagine a series of concentric circles: right in the center is the ancient White Tower; and then there's the Inner Ward, which is enclosed by a massive wall with thirteen towers; and then there's the narrow Outer Ward, protected by a second wall with six towers facing the river and two bastions on the north front. And then there's the moat, which is now a dry moat. There's no water in the moat. Most of us Yeoman Warders live right on the edge, facing the moat, but the ravens are slap-bang in the middle of things. They're based in a purpose-built, state-of-the-art enclosure on the south side of Tower Green, in the Inner Ward. It is the perfect spot, sheltered but warm and sunny, at the center of the life of the Tower but just tucked away enough to give them some privacy. It's on the site of what was once the Grand Hall, which we think was probably where Anne Boleyn was imprisoned before her execution in 1536.

Living here at the Tower, for both the birds and the Yeoman Warders, is just like living anywhere else—apart from the fact that we have arrow slits for windows, our walls are forty feet high, and we're locked in at night!

I suppose I'm used to this sort of thing. I lived in some pretty unusual places during my time in the army. I spent plenty of nights bivouacked in the jungle, and under the stars in the fields of South Armagh. I lived in Cyprus, among the orange trees and the olive groves, and up high in the mountains in the Balkans. When you're a soldier you get used to roughing it—you're at home everywhere and nowhere. The Tower is as peculiar and unexpected a place to live as anywhere.

There are about 140 residents here at the Tower. As well as the Yeoman Warders and their families, the Constable of the Tower lives here, the Resident Governor and Deputy Governor, the chaplain, the doctor, the Operations Manager, the Chief Warden, the head of Visitor Services, and the manager of the Fusilier Museum. We may share our home with millions of visitors every year, but we're a little community just like any other. We have our own doctor, and we even have our own club, the Yeoman Warders Club, the Keys, which is arguably the most exclusive club in the world since it's only open to Tower residents, staff, and invited guests.

Some people would find living in the Tower intolerable. You're basically in the middle of London, in a prime tourist destination, with the public continually passing through. It's like a fishbowl. It's certainly not for everyone. But for me, from the moment I arrived, it felt like coming home.

When I was young we lived in the shadow of Dover Castle. Dover sits facing France across the Channel and is the traditional entry and exit point for visitors from abroad. Home of the famous White Cliffs, Dover is what some people like to think of as the back door into England. I like to think of it as more of a grand entrance. Who knows how much I might have been influenced as a child, looking up at the old Norman castle, floodlit at night, the trains fuming into the station, the endless comings and goings of the ferries? Growing up in Dover I became accustomed to living in a place where people were continually passing through, tourists and travelers on their way in and out of England, and maybe I even had a dim sense of living in a place of great historic importance. I may have come a long way from Dover, but in some ways, I haven't come far at all.

As I mentioned, most of us Yeoman Warders live in the outskirts of the Tower, in the outer walls known as the Casemates, the outer battlements. The ravens live in the very shadow of the White Tower, a building that dominates the whole of the Tower of London even today, a symbol as much as it is a building, built centuries before the "starchitects" and their skyscrapers that surround us now. Decades in construction, the White Tower was begun by William the Conqueror around the late 1070s, with the object of protecting the city and impressing the populace, as well as controlling the approach to London by river. Work on the White Tower was continued by William's son William Rufus and was eventually finished by Henry I around 1100, at which point Henry promptly imprisoned his chief minister, Ranulf Flambard, in the newly completed building, though Flambard soon escaped, climbing down a rope, having plied his guards with drink. You can certainly try that with the Yeoman Warders today. It won't work. But it's certainly worth a try.

When I started as Ravenmaster the ravens were kept in rather cramped night boxes, constructed in the 1980s and built into the old inner walls of the Tower. There was nothing really wrong with the night boxes. They were an improvement on how the ravens were housed before then. According to an article in *Country Life* magazine in December 1955, some of the Tower ravens were "locked in the basement of a house overlooking the Green and others were confined to a cage hung on the side of the Chapel of St. Peter ad Vincula." Remnants of these rather primitive sleeping quarters remain today—and indeed are still in use by Merlina, who refuses to sleep with the other ravens, preferring her own company and a private night box behind an old lead-lined window on the ground floor of the Queen's House on Tower Green, where she graciously allows the Constable of the Tower and his family to live.

•

The window of Merlina's night box originally opened into the large basement of the Queen's House, where coal was once stored, and which was first used to house ravens in 1946, when two ravens named Cora and Corax were put up there, perched on a pile of coal. We certainly don't keep our ravens in coal bunkers anymore. (One of the only times in recent history when the ravens have been kept inside at the Tower was during the avian flu virus in 2006, when tens of millions of birds worldwide died, and millions more were slaughtered to prevent the flu spreading. At that time we removed the ravens for their own safety to the upper Brick Tower on the advice of the vets at London Zoo.)

The old night boxes just didn't feel right to me. Ravens are wild birds who should be able to perch outside. They need to be able to fly back and forth. Like humans, they need freedom. But they also need protection. I strongly believe that if we're going to continue to keep ravens at the Tower we have to make it as welcoming a place for them as possible, an environment that, if not entirely natural, is at least a place where they have room to roam in safety. So, soon after I had taken up the post of Ravenmaster, I discussed with the staff of Historic Royal Palaces—the independent charity that looks after the Tower of London, Hampton Court Palace, the Banqueting House, Kensington Palace, Kew Palace, and Hillsborough Castle—the possibility of constructing some sort of large enclosure that would offer the birds protection at night but that we could leave open during the day, thus enabling them to continue to roam freely outside and socialize with one another but also to enjoy some privacy. (I don't like the word *cage*, by the way. I don't even like the word *aviary*. They're words that

imply capture and containment. I always refer to the ravens'
nighttime quarters as *the enclosure*.) Historic Royal Palaces
were as keen as I was to make improvements to the birds'
living arrangements.

It took us about two years of research and consultation
with London Zoo and Historic England and many other
experts to get the design and development of the enclosure
exactly right. Obtaining the planning permission alone was
quite a feat. Just because we're the Tower doesn't mean we
can make up our own rules. We had to obtain all the same
planning permissions as anyone else. You can perhaps imagine the look on the face of the poor planning officer when our
Planning Service application arrived on their desk: "Erec-
tion of new cages and night boxes for Ravens, HM Tower of
London." The main thing was to get the build right for the
ravens, not just for the Tower or for my benefit or for the benefit
of visitors; it needed to be something that the birds would
want to use as a base.

The enclosure is made out of oak and a special fine wire
which flexes if the birds should accidentally fly into it, to prevent them from getting injured. A tragic entry in the Tower
Orders—which are the records of day-to-day activities at the
Tower—for April 18, 1975, notes that Raven Brora was "Discovered entangled in wiring of the raven's cage. Because of
injuries had to be destroyed." It was of the utmost importance
to me when designing the enclosure that this kind of terrible
accident could never happen again.

One of the main requirements when we were planning

the enclosure is that it had to be absolutely fox-proof. Even now, I'll often arrive in the morning to signs that the foxes have once again attempted to dig under the wire to get at the birds. They have no chance: I made sure that the wire goes straight down into the concrete and hardcore foundations. But you'd be amazed where foxes can get in. They can squeeze through the smallest gap—I've seen them manage to slip through gaps just a few inches wide, and once they're in, they're in and there's absolutely nothing you can do about it. We've lost many a raven to foxes over the years. They sneak in under the drawbridges, crawl through the gutters, and trot through secret passageways. Sometimes I think my job title should be the Fox- and Ravenmaster: I'm engaged in a continual battle just trying to keep them apart.

•

The enclosure has separate areas inside for each bird or pair of birds to be able to sleep, and big sliding doors that allow me to open up the entire space so that they can come and go as they please. Each bird has its own perches and a large night box within the enclosure. All of this might sound straightforward, but it took a long time to work out the design, based on careful observation of the birds' behavior.

As I said, the enclosure is really only for nighttime. The birds are out flying or walking around during the day, all day, every day. Very occasionally I keep them in the enclosure if they need looking after—if they're sick, or if they just need a break. Being on show to the public every day can be exhausting, as we Yeoman Warders know only too well. Sometimes you just need to take some time off to be by yourself and to relax and recharge. I'm always looking for signs of stress in the birds. If I sense that they need a break for whatever reason, I keep them in. I've been living and working with the ravens for such a long time now that I can tell when something's not right, the same as you can tell if your loved ones need some extra attention. You just know. The Tower is a community—and the ravens are an essential part of that community.

6

TOWER GREEN

Now that you have a good sense of where we all live, you'll probably want to know about our daily routine.

The Ravenmaster's basic duties and responsibilities can be summarized thus:

1. Clean and prepare the ravens' water bowls for the day.
2. Clean their enclosures and remove any food they've discarded from the night before.
3. Check each raven closely for any health issues.
4. Feed the ravens; administer any medicines, such as worming tablets; monitor their food intake.
5. Release the ravens from the enclosures for the day.
6. Watch the ravens' movements as they make their way to their territories, checking and recording any wing or leg damage.

7. Monitor the ravens throughout the day, ensuring the safety of both the ravens and the public and dealing with any issues arising.

8. Return the ravens safely to their enclosures at night.

9. Prepare food for the morning.

10. Final check before lights-out.

In theory that's it. Sounds pretty easy, doesn't it? In practice, though, it's a *little* bit more complicated.

For simplicity's sake, let's begin at the beginning. I'm up and out onto Tower Green at the crack of dawn. My first call of the day, every day, is to check on Merlina, since she mostly likes to stay out at night, up on the rooftops. Merlina is the only raven who stays out at night. The other ravens all return to the enclosure on the south side of Tower Green. Merlina refuses to do so. Merlina treats the rooftops around Tower Green as a penthouse suite—a place to retreat and to contemplate the world. Once I can see her silhouette and I can hear her call, I make sure that the whole area around Tower Green is safe and clear from debris or anything that might harm the birds. And then I proceed to fill the water bowls.

This might sound silly, but I love filling the water bowls. It's one of the highlights of my day. I scrub and refill the bowls daily. There are plastic water bowls in the raven enclosures and six stone bowls dotted around the Tower's Inner Ward where the ravens spend their days. I like the simple act of refilling the bowls, the sound of it, the smell of it, the clarity

of the water. It's a ritual for me. It's my quiet time. This is
when I get to clear my head and think about the day. They
say that getting up and out early in the morning into the
fresh air, no matter what the season, is good for your mental
and physical health. All I can say is that I've been up and out
early in all seasons every day for my entire working life, and
so far so good.

There's one water bowl which is up on the north side of
Tower Green, by the Chapel of St. Peter ad Vincula. It's believed that there may have been a place of worship there for
over a thousand years, predating even the White Tower. Some
even claim that this part of London is one of the nation's ancient holy places, our own little central London Glastonbury
or Stonehenge. And legend has it that there was once a spring
of fresh water up at Tower Hill, the site of a sacred mound,
and you get druids turning up these days in their costumes
to celebrate the spring equinox, though I've never been
tempted myself. According to Celtic legend, around here is
also where the head of Brân the Blessed, the king of England
in Welsh mythology, was buried. Brân means "raven" and
he's supposed to have been buried not far from the ravens'
current enclosures, which seems appropriate. (Bran is also
of course the name of a character in the series of novels by
George R. R. Martin, *A Song of Ice and Fire*, and its famous
television adaptation, *Game of Thrones*. But more about
Mr. Martin and the ravens later.)

I've heard it said that the name of London derives
from Lugdunum, from the Celtic Lugdon, meaning town of

ravens—mind you, I've also heard that the name comes from Llyn-don, Laindon, Karelundein, Caer Ludd, Lundunes, Lindonion, Lundene, Lundone, Ludenberk, Longidinium, and goodness knows what else. History and prehistory, legends, fables, and stories, they're everywhere here. I sometimes think that the Tower is just a vast storehouse of the human imagination, and the ravens are its guardians.

Anyway, I refill the bowl by St. Peter ad Vincula, where generations of Tower residents have been baptized—not in the ravens' water bowl, I might add!—and married and, most famously, buried, including Sir Thomas More, Bishop Fisher, Queen Anne Boleyn, Queen Catherine Howard, and Lady Jane Grey, the uncrowned Queen of only nine days. Quite a few of them were also executed near the Chapel, or within the walls of the Tower—Anne Boleyn, of course, and Catherine Howard, Lady Jane Grey, Margaret Pole, Robert Devereux— so it's certainly a church with a colorful history, though I've always thought the historian Thomas Macaulay was a bit down on the place in his *History of England*:

> In truth there is no sadder spot on the earth. . . . Death is there associated, not, as in Westminster Abbey and Saint Paul's, with genius and virtue, with public veneration and imperishable renown; not, as in our humblest churches and churchyards, with everything that is most endearing in social and domestic chari- ties; but with whatever is darkest in human nature and in human destiny, with the savage triumph of

implacable enemies, with the inconstancy, the in-
gratitude, the cowardice of friends, with all the mis-
eries of fallen greatness and of blighted fame.

It's not that bad! I rather like the chapel. It's our parish
church, after all, with a chaplain to guide and direct our spir-
itual lives and a fine choir and organists to lead the worship
and uplift our spirits. Though, to be honest, I prefer to say my
prayers outside, with brush and bucket in hand.

Fresh water sorted, brush and bucket safely stowed, every
morning I then make my way to unlock the storeroom
where I keep all of the food and equipment needed to aid me
in looking after the ravens. I walk under the archway of the
Bloody Tower onto the old cobbles of Water Lane (so-called
because this is where the water of the Thames used to lap
up against the walls of the Tower). Water Lane is part of
Edward I's Outer Ward, which was created during his big
expansion program in the thirteenth century. It was reclaimed
from the river by sinking thousands of beech piles into the
Thames mud. I like having the storeroom here. I've always
thought that back in the day Water Lane would have been
full of wheelers and dealers, and duckers and divers coming
in and out of the Tower and the old pubs that used to be
here—the Stone Kitchen tavern was one, shut down by the
Duke of Wellington long ago. The Tower has *always* been full
of people, inside and out, and the Ravenmaster's storeroom
just sort of fits here, right in the thick of things, behind its
own ancient black door, like an old apothecary's shop.

Like all the other Yeoman Warders, on my key ring I keep a whistle to alert the others if there's a problem. Plus I have a little skull and crossbones memento mori—you can't work with ravens and not develop a bit of a taste for the macabre—and a small wooden raven totem pole, which I keep as a kind of talisman.

Now let me open up the storeroom and show you the Ravenmaster's inner sanctum.

7

BISCUITS AND BLOOD

I like to keep the storeroom neat and tidy at all times, the result no doubt of a lifetime in the military. When you join the army as a young recruit you're taught everything, and I mean *everything*. You learn how to clean your teeth and how to make your bed and tie your boots, how to iron and fold your clothes. Above all, you're taught never to just leave stuff lying around. It's drilled into you. You survive by following routines and procedures. A place for everything and everything in its place. No excuses.

So in the storeroom there's the fridge, the freezer, the sink, and the countertops, all kept spick-and-span. Raven calendar on the wall, obviously, and our daily diary underneath it, so the whole team can keep up-to-date and log what's happening with the birds. There's the fishing net on its shelf, used for raven-catching purposes, if a raven is injured and needs immediate veterinary attention. Chasing a raven around the Tower in full view of the public, fishing net in hand, like the child catcher from *Chitty Chitty Bang Bang*—believe me, that really is an experience. The first-aid kit: you certainly know if you've had a nip from a raven. Scales for weighing the birds, which we do once a month. Chopping boards and equipment for preparing the meals. Rubber gloves. Leather falconry gloves. Metal gauntlets—which I do not recommend for handling the ravens, because they do sometimes like to try to crush your fingers, and picking metal out of flesh is never nice, as I can testify. A couple of wooden boxes to carry sick birds to the vets we work with at London Zoo. There's also an old plastic KerPlunk, which we like to use for the ravens' entertainment. (In KerPlunk: The Raven Edition, the challenge for the birds is to remove the straws in order to win a dead mouse, which we place on top of the straws, ready to fall down and be eaten. Good clean raven fun. Munin is the reigning champion.) I also keep a jar full of raven feathers in the storeroom, kindly donated by the ravens once a year during their molt, and which I occasionally like to distribute to deserving/well-behaved/lucky visitors. If I'm doing a Tower tour, for example, and I discover that a couple just got married or engaged, I like to give them a pair of feathers—a primary and a secondary, since without one the other is no good. I'm an old romantic at heart. Sometimes people request feathers for use as quills, or for medicinal purposes, or for musical instruments, though exactly which musical instruments or for what medicinal purposes I'm not entirely sure, or indeed whether raven feathers make particularly good quills.

•

As the Ravenmaster you get used to fielding all sorts of bizarre requests and questions from the public. No, you cannot buy the birds. No, you cannot sponsor them. And no, you cannot borrow them. They belong to the Tower: or the Tower belongs to them. In case you're interested, here are the top five questions that people tend to ask us Yeoman Warders, and the sorts of answers we like to give:

1. *"Where's the bathroom?"*
Usually asked by our American visitors, who—may I say—are unfailingly charming and polite. Alas, in British English we tend to rather crudely refer to what Americans call the bathroom as the "toilet," and to us a bathroom is the place you go to have a bath, so we tend to reply, "Why, sir, do you need a bath?"

2. *"Where are the instruments of torture?"*
Answers to this one vary from Yeoman Warder to Yeoman Warder, but they tend to go along the lines of "Try working here every day and you'll soon find out."

3. *"Where was Anne Boleyn executed?"*
This one demands the obvious answer, "Somewhere around the neck area, sir."

4. *"Have you ever seen a ghost?"*
Some Yeoman Warders like to use this question as a prompt to tell the classic tales about the boy princes,

the headless apparitions, Sir Walter Raleigh on the battlements, and all the other chain-rattling Victorian nonsense. My preferred response tends to be something like, "No, sir, but we certainly keep plenty of spirits in our clubhouse."

5. *"Who built the Tower?"*

The Tower was built over the course of several centuries (though the medieval defenses are essentially unchanged), so this question can elicit all sorts of responses, ranging from the patriotic "As well to ask, sir, who built the spirit of the Great British people!" to "Well, we haven't quite finished it yet, but we're getting there," to a fully comprehensive explanation of the major enlargements and extensions to the building undertaken by Edward III and Richard II during the fourteenth century, to the confusing but accurate "Either 1075, 1078, or 1080, depending on which historical sources you consult." I prefer to explain that the Tower was founded by William the Conqueror and that the building of the great White Tower in stone was probably supervised by the Bishop of Rochester, Gundulf of Bec, who is not to be confused with Gandalf the Grey.

To be honest, the answers all rather depend on what day of the week it is, but basically, if you keep setting 'em up, we'll keep knocking 'em down.

•

Anyway, as I was saying, that's basically the storeroom. Except, of course, for the dog biscuits. Bag upon bag upon row upon row of dog biscuits, all neatly lined up on the shelves. When people ask if they can come and see the ravens, or if there's a group who want to come and talk to me about them, I have one simple request and requirement: that they bring with them a bag of dog biscuits. This is absolutely nonnegotiable. I like to think that our ravens have the best diet of any bird in the world, a proper varied diet which keeps them strong and healthy. But everyone deserves a treat now and then, and the ravens love a nice dog biscuit soaked in blood. To prepare biscuits in blood, you simply place the dog biscuits into a container filled with blood and leave to soak for at least an hour—the longer the better. *Et voilà! Bon appétit!*

Rats are also a bit of a treat for the birds. I buy rats in bulk from a specialist supplier and store them in the freezer. Then I get out what I need the night before, defrost them in the fridge, and prepare them in the morning. A nice fat rat'll do a raven all day. A raven's preferred method of engagement with a dead rat, or indeed with a live mouse if they get hold of one, is perfectly straightforward: foot on, claws in, beak engaged, guts first, then the rest stripped bare, leaving just the skin. All that usually remains is what looks like a mini ratskin rug, which I like to bag up for the Tower foxes so there's no waste.

The ravens get through about a ton and a half of food a

year. Their diet mostly consists of chicken, lamb and pig hearts, liver, kidney, mice, rats, day-old chicks, peanuts in their shells, the occasional boiled egg, and some fish, steak chunks, and rabbit (with the fur left on). Anything else they want, they steal it from the bins and from the public, or they just go out and kill it. Most of the meat I get from Smithfield Market. If you've never been to Smithfield Market, you should go before it's too late. It's one of the great old London institutions, a proper wholesale market, but also open to the public, and always under threat of being redeveloped and turned into swanky offices and fancy restaurants. Smithfield is not for the fainthearted. I was a regular for about a year before any of the traders deigned to actually give me a nod, never mind speak to me. You can get amazing bargains, though only if you're there by about 5:00 a.m. at the latest, and if you're prepared to buy in bulk. Whatever you do, don't ask for a single lamb chop. Tell the lads there that I sent you. They'll probably tell you where to go, but nonetheless. It's a start. And once you're there you might as well nip into The Hope for a pint, or La Forchetta for a cup of tea and a fry-up.

(Personally, I don't like to eat until I've fed the ravens in the morning. This is not out of politeness. It's not a matter of manners. I don't know if you've tossed many rats to a raven, or if you've ever had to clear up yesterday's mauled meat leftovers, but from my experience you really don't want to be doing so while digesting an early morning bacon sandwich. Trust me, it's best to go with a bowl of porridge once the job is over and done with.)

To be honest, I'd probably prefer if the birds were all vegetarian, but ravens, like a lot of us humans, are meat eaters. There's a theory that we Yeoman Warders got the nickname Beefeaters because as members of the royal bodyguard we were permitted to eat as much beef as we could from the king's table. There are plenty of other theories about the origin of the nickname, but whether any of them are conclusive evidence I don't know. Frankly, we all prefer to be called Yeoman Warders anyway.

Given a choice, I fancy that many of the ravens, like many of us, would probably survive on junk food. Merlina in particular is very partial to a potato chip. She watches out for any little chip that a young visitor might drop from her lunch bag, and she'll take it to one of the water bowls and give it a good rinse, softening it up for consumption. She has a particular ability to be able to spot a tube of Pringles from the other side of Tower Green, hop right up to an innocent member of the public, steal the whole tube, hop off with it, pop off the lid, and quickly cram as many chips into her mouth as she possibly can before being noticed! This is worth bearing in mind if you're thinking of visiting the Tower and bringing a snack with you. Remember: ravens are opportunists and will happily steal *anything* from you if and when the need arises.

I have spent almost as many years now standing at my post on Tower Green watching the ravens getting into scrapes as I spent getting into scrapes myself in the army, and I can safely say that to watch a raven at work scavenging food is to witness something very much like a military operation. As a soldier you're taught all sorts of drills and standard operating procedures to prepare for battle and how to analyze your options when engaged on a mission. In military terms this is how we might describe one of Merlina's typical sandwich-snatch operations:

MISSION: To steal a ham sandwich from a visitor sitting on a bench.

PLAN OF ATTACK: Sneak up from the rear with stealth and cunning, hide under the bench until the target puts down the sandwich, then remove the prize by pulling at it through the bench slats until in full possession. Then hop off.

ACTIONS ON: If detected on the approach to the bench, look innocent and peck at the ground.

ACTIONS ON: If member of the public isn't putting the sandwich down, jump on the bench and scare them until they drop it.

ACTIONS ON: If unable to tug the sandwich through the bench slat, pull harder and store as much as you can in your mouth at the same time.

RE-ORG: Hop to the Ravenmaster for protection while you're being chased by the angry visitor.

Whatever their personal snacking habits, I always feed the ravens in the enclosure twice a day, once in the morning and then sometime in the afternoon. Feeding them in the en-

closure allows me to monitor what they're eating. In the past
the Ravenmasters preferred to put the food out around the
Tower, but the problem was that a seagull might take a
nice juicy piece of ox liver, say, that was intended for a raven,
have a little nibble on it and then casually drop it on a visitor
from a great height. I've seen it happen more than once, and
believe me, it is not a pretty sight. These days the ravens have
come to expect to find food in the enclosure, and because they
know they're going to be fed safely there, they're happy to
roam around all day. It also encourages them to go back to the
enclosure as the light fades. It's a win-win.

In preparing the food, it's important of course that we
follow basic health and safety requirements. I am an absolute stickler for proper hand-washing procedures. Plus, I like
the smell of all the antiseptic stuff. I can remember when I'd
just started work at the Tower and the old Ravenmaster,
Derrick Coyle, would walk into our guardroom, the Yeoman
Warders' Hall, and I could smell the antiseptic on him. It
always reminded me of my childhood. The smell of my mum
scrubbing up in the hairdressing salon where she worked,
the smell of a day having been properly completed, or just
begun. The smell of cleanliness, of preparedness, of a job
well done.

•

Once I've distributed the food to the birds in the enclosure,
I leave them for an hour or so before letting them out. The
great thing about ravens, unlike, say, us humans, is that they'll

only eat until they've had enough and then they like to go off and exercise. Anything they don't use, they'll cache.

And speaking of caching, the next thing I do every morning is take care of the foxes.

If there's one thing I've learned in a life dealing with animals, it's this: there are always foxes to be taken care of.

8

THE MENAGERIE

As Ravenmaster, I see myself as responsible for all the wild-life in the Tower—including the foxes. What I've tried to do here over the years is to create a balance between everyone's competing needs: the ravens, the foxes, the Yeoman Warders, the Tower visitors. We all share the environment of the Tower, and my job is really about finding ways to enable us to live in harmony together. Most of the time all it requires is a bit of forethought and some careful husbandry. If you leave food lying around, for example—guess what?—the foxes come in where you don't want them, and they can cause ab-solute havoc. In the old days, of course, we'd just catch and cage the foxes and take them away for extermination, but my feel-ing is that they have *almost* as much right to be here as the rest of us.

In order to maintain our modest little ecosystem here, every morning after I've fed the ravens I take any scraps of food to the fox cache. A cache is a hiding place for ammunition, food, or indeed treasure of any sort. In the army we were taught to set up caches in evasion and recovery operations, storing food and water or medical items, communication equipment, that sort of thing. I decided to set up the fox cache a few years ago when I realized that the best way to manage the foxes in the Tower was to try to think like a fox. It's that old military thing: know your enemy. With foxes you have to understand that they really just want to come and fill their bellies, and then they're happy and they'll leave you alone. So I found a special place where I can deliver food to them every day, which keeps them happy and well away from the ravens' enclosure. Job done.

(And how did I know the best place to leave the food for the foxes? you might ask. Well, I probably know every nook and cranny in the Tower, every rooftop and gutter, every walkway, every staircase, every little crack and fissure. Wherever it is, however high or low, however inaccessible, I've been there, found the ravens hiding there, found something they've hidden there, or found a fox's hole or nest or den or warren. Visitors are always asking about hidden tunnels in the Tower. All I can say is that I've never discovered any—and I've been looking for years.)

The Tower throughout its history has always been a place full of all sorts of animals. These days a lot of those animals are the cats and dogs and other pets owned by the Yeoman Warders—you'd be surprised how many of us are out early in the morning, walking our dogs in the moat. Apart from the ravens and the foxes, there are also the various squirrels, seagulls, pigeons, sparrows, starlings, kestrels, blue tits, crows, mice, rats, and even the odd pair of Egyptian geese that like to stop over and drink from the ravens' water bowls. The Tower is an eighteen-acre green oasis in the middle of London, after all. We have a breeding pair of kestrels in one of the arrow slits opposite my house in the Casemates, who have been resident now for many years; we have four different kinds of bats; and every year when Traitors' Gate is full of water we usually get a duck family settling in with their ducklings. Two magpies, whom I call Ronnie and Reggie Kray after the notorious 1960s London gangsters, like to visit the ravens' enclosure looking for scraps of leftover meat and seem to have been accepted by them—perhaps on the threat of violence, who knows.

Until relatively recently, though, most of the animals in the Tower would have been the exotic beasts presented by the rulers of faraway lands to the kings and queens of England. For more than six hundred years the Tower was a sort of a zoo, or at least a storehouse for rare creatures of all kinds, who were an entertainment and spectacle for the Tower's visitors. In a sense, the ravens are another chapter in the great Royal Menagerie story, and the Ravenmaster is a zookeeper of the world's only single-species open-air zoo.

The term *menagerie*—which I like to use to refer to *all* of us who live and work together in the Tower—derives from the French and refers to an aristocratic or royal collection of captive animals. As every schoolchild knows, when William the Conqueror invaded in 1066 he ordered that a series of fortresses be built around England to protect his barons from the threat of invading armies and civil dissent—among which fortresses the Tower is of course only the most famous and most long-standing. According to the Domesday Book, the Normans founded nearly fifty castles in the twenty years after landing at Hastings, a building program unprecedented in English history, and which makes even the current real estate boom in London seem not so much a bang as a whimper. What's perhaps less well-known is that William's son Henry established England's first menagerie at his manor house in Oxford, building a big wall to contain his collection of lions, camels, and porcupines. This small royal zoo was eventually moved to the Tower around 1204, during the reign of King John, and hence the beginning of the Royal Menagerie.

There have of course always been famous animals who have called London home. When I was growing up it was Chi-Chi and Ching-Ching, the giant pandas at London Zoo, and Guy the gorilla. Earlier in the twentieth century there was Winnie, the female Canadian black bear who was apparently the inspiration for Winnie-the-Pooh. And back in the nineteenth century there was the mighty Obaysch, the first hippo in Europe since the days of the Roman Empire, who caused a sensation: Queen Victoria came to watch him swimming in Regent's Park and compared him to a porpoise. But before all of them, there were the animals of the Tower, the bigger and stranger the better.

There was a white bear, for example—possibly a polar bear—who was a gift from King Haakon IV of Norway to

King Henry III in 1252, and who was kept tethered at the riverside with a huge collar and long rope, allowing him to fish for food in the Thames. I like to imagine the look upon the faces of anyone that happened to be sailing up or down the river when they saw a big white bear swimming past! In addition, in 1255, King Louis IX of France gave King Henry III an African elephant. Just getting it to London must have been a logistical nightmare. According to one eyewitness, "The people flocked to see the novel sight. . . . The beast is about ten years old, possessing a rough hide rather than fur, has small eyes at the top of its head, and eats and drinks with a trunk." Again, what a sight, to have seen an elephant at the Tower back then: I compare it today to seeing a *Tyrannosaurus rex* or some sort of animatronic giant suddenly poking its head over the battlements.

Like any great collection, the Royal Menagerie just grew and grew, and by the 1300s all the animals in the Tower had to be moved outside to the main western entrance, which was later named the Lion Tower, for obvious reasons. By the time Edward I came to the throne, an official position had been created known as Keeper of the Lions and Leopards, later renamed the Master of the King's Bears and Apes.

(My absolute favorite menagerie story is about Elizabeth I, who, as was customary, spent the night before her coronation procession at the Tower. It is said that as the great procession left the Tower to travel through the streets of London to Westminster Abbey, she stopped to deliver a speech to the assembled crowds and to pray to God for her safety. "Thou hast dealt as wonderfully and mercifully with me," said Elizabeth, "as Thou didst with Daniel, whom Thou delivered from the cruelty of raging lions"—at which moment it is reported that a great roar of the Tower's lions could be heard, to the astonishment and delight of the crowd. I rather suspect a bit of careful Tower stage management here, with the Keeper of the Lions and Leopards, a man called Ralph Worsley, perhaps ready with the script of Elizabeth's speech in one hand and a glowing red-hot poker in the other, red-hot pokers being used at the time to control the lions. Statecraft, after all, is a form of stagecraft.)

•

It wasn't until 1831 that most of the animals kept in the Tower were transferred to the recently established London Zoo in Regent's Park, the rest of them being sold off to the American showman P. T. Barnum for his famous touring circus. And it was then in 1835, on the orders of the Duke of Wellington, the Constable of the Tower, that the Royal Menagerie was finally closed. Although the first Ravenmaster wasn't officially appointed until the late 1960s, I like to think we kind of carry on in the tradition of the ancient Keepers of the Lions and Leopards, though of course they didn't exactly look after the animals according to the standards that we might expect today.

There were monkeys, apparently, who were kept in fully furnished rooms. There was a leopard who used to be baited with umbrellas and parasols thrust through the bars of its cage, and there was a zebra who was said to have enjoyed a beer on occasion, and who would duly be served a pint or two in the old soldiers' canteen. Even today I'm often surprised at what some of our guests think our ravens might like to eat and drink. Just for the record, ravens, though omnivorous, should not and do not eat any of the following items: bubble gum, cola cubes, paper, cigarette butts, chocolate, toffee, or children's fingers. All of which I have seen being offered up to the ravens on an almost daily basis during my time at the Tower!

The lesson of the Tower's menagerie—and certainly the lesson of my own experience with the Tower foxes—seems to be that if we treat animals with respect, we can expect the same in return.

9

BLACK BIRDS

In order to help members of the public identify the birds and for my team to be able to keep an eye on them if I'm not around, the ravens usefully wear colored anklets. I've trained them to put them on every morning, just like we put on our shoes and socks. No, of course I haven't! But for the record, at the time of writing, Munin wears lime green, Jubilee II gold, Gripp II light blue, Harris purple, Rocky brown, Erin red, and Merlina of course bright pink.

Most of us city dwellers these days can identify a pigeon—they're absolutely everywhere—and a blackbird and a robin. A duck, maybe, as long as we don't have to confirm what kind of a duck. But that's probably about it on a day-to-day basis. Before I became the Ravenmaster I wouldn't have been able to identify too many birds either, so let me provide you with a basic guide to raven identification: the Ravenmaster's Guide to Raven Spotting.

First, let's get our terms correct. Some of the local names

we have for ravens in the U.K. and Ireland include corbie, corby, croupy craw, croupie, in Irish *fiach* or *bran*, in Cornwall *marburan*, revein, parson, Ralph, and in Welsh, *cigfran*, *cigfrain*, *gigfran*. Common names of the raven worldwide include:

Danish: *ravn*
French: *corbeau*
German: *Rabe*
Italian: *corvo*
Japanese: *karasu*
Polish: *kruk*
Russian: *ворон (voron)*
Spanish: *cuervo*
Turkish: *kuzgun*

Working at the Tower, you get to pick up all sorts of lingo: I know the word for "exit" in all the major European languages, in Arabic, and in Brazilian Portuguese, as well as the international sign language for "lavatory" (or what Americans call "the bathroom"). Whatever you happen to call them, the ravens at the Tower are what are properly, Latinly called *Corvus corax*, as named by Carl Linnaeus, who—you'll remember if you listened in your science lessons in school, which I certainly did not—was the Swedish biologist who came up with the whole system of naming species.

Ravens are part of the corvid family of birds, which includes crows, magpies, jays, nutcrackers, and even cute little choughs. In Britain and Ireland, the most common corvids are *Corvus frugilegus*, the rooks, with their gray faces and rounded tail feathers; carrion crows, *Corvus corona*, who have shorter beaks than the rooks; hooded crows, *Corvus cornix*, which are the ones that look like they're wearing gray jumpers or hoodies; *Corvus pica*, or *Pica pica*, the magpie, who needs no introduction; and jackdaws, *Corvus monedula*, those strange stubby little creatures with mad staring silvery eyes. Blackbirds, note, are *not* corvids: they are thrushes. A lot of corvids are black birds, but not all black birds are corvids. I know, it's confusing. But don't blame me. I didn't make up the rules.

There are more than forty members of the genus *Corvus* worldwide, and they all tend to be, in general and in summary, adaptable, intelligent birds who typically mate for life, hide their surplus food, and eat both animals and vegetables. They're also an incredibly hardy bunch who can be found just about anywhere and are at home anywhere— in deserts, in the Arctic, on coasts, on mountain peaks and in towns and cities. Ravens are survivors.

They're also sleek. They are stocky. They have strong legs and feet, and a distinctive gait which makes them seem rather human: they walk with a sort of a roll and a slouch. Charles Dickens described their walk as like that "of a very particular gentleman with exceedingly tight boots on, trying to walk fast over loose pebbles." I couldn't put it better myself. They also have large heads and large eyes proportionate to their bodies. They have stout heavy bills and they're a little bit shaggy and jowly around the throat—like a lot of Yeoman Warders, in fact. They look a bit like crows, but they are bigger than crows. Quite a lot bigger. Ravens weigh about *three times* as much as your average crow, which is more than the difference between a light flyweight and a heavyweight in boxing. That's a big difference. Their beaks are bigger and heavier than a crow's, and they have a broader wingspan—a raven's wingspan is between three and four feet. How else can you tell the difference between a raven and a crow? Ravens often fly in pairs: crows usually fly in groups. A raven's tail is wedge-shaped: a crow's tail is more like a fan. Ravens croak: crows caw.

The first time I got up close and personal with the ravens I couldn't believe the size of them. I had been working at the Tower for about six months when the Ravenmaster at the time, Derrick Coyle, came up to me and said, "Hey, Boy!" He called everyone Boy. He was about sixty at the time. I was about forty. "Hey, Boy," he said, "I think the ravens might like you."

I wasn't entirely sure whether Derrick meant that they might like me, as in they would like to *eat* me, or whether they would like me as a person or as a Yeoman Warder. I had visions of something like *Strictly Come Dancing*, with the birds all lined up holding scorecard marks out of ten. Whatever he meant, I was intrigued. Since arriving at the Tower I'd watched the ravens hopping around Tower Green, going about their daily business, but I had no real understanding of exactly why they were here or what they did. I knew almost nothing about birds. At school I'd had a friend who was a keen pigeon racer and I remember he showed me his pigeons once, which I'll be honest I wasn't that excited about. My only real contact with the Tower ravens was when our cat, a large gray Persian called Tigger, used to bother them by sitting on top of the old cages, lazily dangling his paw through the bars and teasing them, and Derrick would yell at me, "Get that dammed cat off the cages, Chris, or the birds will have it for dinner!" Surely, I thought, it should be the other way around? Years later, of course I've realized just how right Derrick was: more than once I've seen a raven chasing the Tower's many resident cats and dogs.

"Come on then," said Derrick. "Follow me." And I followed. You did not argue with Derrick Coyle, RVM (Royal Victorian Medal). He'd been a legend in the army and he was a legend within the body of Yeoman Warders. With Derrick, what you saw was what you jolly well got. He'd had an exemplary military career, having joined the Green Howards—a famous British Infantry unit, also known as the Yorkshire Regiment—as a boy soldier and having worked his way up the ranks to become the battalion's RSM (Regimental Sergeant Major). He was your archetypal Sergeant Major, tall and erect even when relaxed, always smart, always sharp. He would have been perfect in an old black-and-white war movie. But beneath his harsh military exterior he was the very kindest of gentlemen, and a great judge of character.

So Derrick led me to the old raven quarters, opened up the door, and told me to get inside the cage with two of the biggest birds that I had ever seen.

"Don't look them directly in the eye," he said. "And keep

your distance. Don't get too close. They find it threatening."
They find it threatening! I had absolutely no intention of looking them directly in the eye or getting too close!

I was feeling rather intimidated. I'd always been keen on wildlife, but I'd never been this close to such huge birds before and I didn't quite know what to expect. Anyone who's ever been trapped in a small space with a bird will know exactly what I mean: you don't have to be ornithophobic to be a little bit anxious around birds. If you don't know what you're doing, and you don't understand what *they're* doing, birds can seem wildly unpredictable. I'd also heard from the other Yeoman Warders all sorts of lurid tales of raven attacks and the last thing I wanted was to be bitten.

I edged very slowly further inside the cage.

"Don't show them you're scared," said Derrick. "They'll notice, and they'll remember."

"Okay," I said, absolutely petrified, but determined not to show it.

So there I was, standing in the corner of the cage for what seemed like an eternity, with a pair of ravens staring hard at me, their beady eyes piercing deep into my soul. I've been in some tricky spots in my time, but I can remember that as if it were yesterday. Suddenly, to my surprise one of the birds came and perched right next to me. I could feel the raven's breath on my face. I wondered whether I should start to move away slowly, but to my surprise the raven simply cocked its head from side to side, then dipped its head as if to bow, thrust out its wings, and gave a loud cronking sound.

"All right," said Derrick. "Out you come."

Looking back, I realize that Derrick put me in the cage that night with two of the largest ravens to gauge my reaction, to see whether I showed fear and whether I could cope with being around them. Plus, ravens themselves are great judges of character, and Derrick would have picked up instantly whether or not they were going to be able to work with me. Sometimes the only way to learn is to be thrown in at the deep end.

"Yep, you'll do," he said, hauling me out of the cage. "Meet me tomorrow at 0530 hours." And that was that. I'd passed the interview with the ravens and was immediately taken under Derrick's wing as one of the Ravenmaster's assistants. Of course, I wouldn't dream of introducing my new assistants to the ravens like that nowadays. Well, maybe not *quite* like that.

As I was saying, ravens are *big*. The average raven is about two feet long, and they weigh about two and a half pounds. They are indeed the largest of all the so-called passerine birds, which—going back to the naming and classification system—are birds of the order Passeriformes, which includes more than half of all bird species. There are lots of birds that are bigger, obviously—herons and waterfowl, falcons and other birds of prey—but for most of us on a daily basis the corvids are going to be the biggest birds around. And while we're talking Passeriformes, here's a bit more ornithological stuff for you: passerines are divided into three suborders, one of which is called the Passeri, or oscines. "Oscine" means "songbird," and "passerine" literally means "perching." So ravens are part of the corvid family, the oscine suborder, and the passerine order. Which is good to know, isn't it? And which is about all I know about the order Passeriformes. What I can tell you with certainty, passerine-wise, is that perch the ravens most certainly do—often in the most inconvenient of places. Ravens are also elegant and playful in flight, known for their rolls and dives, and when they walk, they like to strut and stride. Oh, and of course their main distinguishing feature is that they are black.

I say they're black, but up close their blackness reveals itself to be an incredible range of deep purples and greens and blues. The feathers of the older ravens in particular become iridescent: Munin and Merlina are astonishingly colorful up close. Over the years I've taken thousands of photos of the ravens to share on social media, and occasionally I manage to catch some of the colors, colors so startling that people sometimes ask if the photos have been altered in some way. Some birds in the corvid family are indeed extremely colorful— the green jay, found in North and South America, for example, is about as bright as a parrot—but even the humble raven contains within its blackness a whole spectrum, a whole rainbow, a chord of black. The black can be sooty, soily, glazed, cindery, blackboard black, kohl black, coal black, *noir, schwarz, nero*. I don't know how many words and phrases there are to describe black—slate black, cast-iron black, jet black, flat-screen-TV black, ink black, burnt black, liturgical black, hell black—but the raven's black is as various and as a dense as there are meanings and values attached to the very idea of black, black representing death, mourning, negation, sin, solemnity, the vacancy of space, and all the horrors of human terror and the exercise of power.

There are many myths and stories about how the ravens and other corvids became black. In Greek myth, Apollo turned a crow from white to black after the bird gave him the bad news that his girlfriend had gone and married someone else. There's also the story of how the prophet Muhammad was hiding from his enemies in a cave when a crow, who was white, spotted him and cried *"Ghar, ghar!"* which means "Cave, cave!" Muhammad's enemies didn't understand the crow's cries, however, and Muhammad duly escaped, but not before he turned the crow black for his betrayal and cursed him forever to only be able to cry "Ghar, ghar!" The Alaskan Athabascans—some of the early inhabitants of Alaska—believed that in the time before humans, when the world was young, the raven was as white as snow. Raven was the creator of the mountains and a lover of life whose soul was filled with light and beauty. All this goodness made his evil black twin brother jealous, and the evil twin killed the white raven—and ever since the world has been imperfect and the raven black. In one of Aesop's Fables a raven desires to be white like a swan and goes to wash his feathers in a lake—but because he's not a swan and he cannot feed there, he drowns!

As far as I can tell, all of the stories about how the raven became black suggest that it was a punishment due to some sort of offense or misdemeanor. Yet in fact, in the wild, black feathers are strong and practical: they absorb heat, which means the birds can live in cold climates as well as in warm, and at night it obviously means that they are indistinguishable, to us and to all other predators. Black is not only beautiful, it is eminently sensible.

10

THE RAVEN
SPREADS HIS WINGS

When we release the ravens from their enclosure in the morning we have to do it in a particular order. Munin and Jubilee go first: they go straight to their territory in the northeast corner of the Tower, by Martin Tower. Then Harris and Gripp: they go to the south lawn. And finally, Erin and Rocky, to the south lawn also: they're the dominant pair, so I always let them out last, which allows the others to get safely to their territories without being challenged by Erin or Rocky en route. If we release the ravens in any other order it causes havoc. And I mean chaos. Mayhem. Ravens are creatures of habit and often the slightest change will cause all sorts of problems. I believe the correct term to describe such a tendency in animal behavior is *neophobic*. They like their rituals and routines. They like their pecking order. They like to know who's who and what's what. I suppose I'm the same.

I watch the ravens every day as they take flight every

morning, during the day, at night, again and again and again. I have watched them and thought about it and studied it thousands of times, and it is a spectacle that never ceases to amaze. They all move slightly differently, of course, every bird, the same as we all move differently depending on our life experiences and our genetic makeup. But they all sort of crouch and then they unfurl their wings and jump, and then they're away, with their wings on a downstroke, which creates the pressure to allow them to move forward and upward, and they flap and flap—but not like a crow's flap, mind you, crows have to make so much effort, while the ravens just glide—and they're away before you know it. It's incredible. You have to slow it down in your mind's eye in order to be able to understand it and to appreciate it, the sight of it, the sound of it. Can you imagine it, that feeling? Can you imagine what it would be like to be able to take off and swoop and glide wherever you wanted, spiraling in the sky without a care in the world, watching the earth below shrink into insignificance, entirely in control of your own destiny? It is one of the great sadnesses of my life that I will never know what it's like to fly.

I do know what it's like to fall. I did my skydiving training with the army in Cyprus. We did a lot of adventure training there: rock climbing, scuba diving, free-fall parachuting. You name it, I've probably done it. It's one of the great perks of being in the army—it's what I joined up for. I was always the sort of soldier who wanted to try everything. I always wanted to see how far I could push myself, how far I could go. I've always been competitive, right from when I was a child. I can remember once I was lined up at the start of a race on sports day at my primary school and I saw my mum in the crowd and I called out, "Mum, watch me win this!" And win it I did. I was the same throughout my military career, always giving things my best shot, as it were. That's just who I am. I've always wanted to test myself, to better myself. During my time as a junior soldier I became a junior lance corporal and then a junior corporal. Not that I was anything special: I was just the sort of soldier who kept on going. I can remember, in training, jumping from the back of a four-tonner—the trusty old British Army trucks used to transport troops and supplies—during one exercise, and I felt my ankle crack, but I was so determined not to be back-squadded I just strapped it up and carried on. About a week later, when I could hardly walk, I finally went to see the doctor. I was put in a plaster cast for six weeks, but even then I kept on training. I couldn't admit defeat.

Watching the ravens, I can well remember my first freefall parachute jump. We were up in a little Cessna, and it came to my turn and I got up and turned around and gave a big thumbs-up and jumped out backward, which we weren't supposed to do. I just thought, why not? I had no fear. My instructor was absolutely furious because I hadn't followed procedures. But it turned out okay: I was the top skydiver in our platoon and was soon asked to join the regimental freefall skydiving team. Alas, my OC—Officer Commanding—at the time had other plans for me, so it never came to be. Instead, I've gotten to live out my fantasy of flying by watching the birds.

All our ravens can fly. The great risk, of course, is that they might fly away. This is the real challenge for the Ravenmaster: how to allow the birds to be as free and as wild as possible, yet to encourage them to remain here at the Tower. It's a balancing act, and one that I've struggled with over the years.

•

In the old days the Ravenmasters used to trim both the primary and secondary flight feathers of one wing on all the birds. (Primary feathers are the largest of the flight feathers and help propel the birds in flight. The secondary feathers help sustain the birds in flight.) Trimming the wings in this way effectively grounded the ravens, which is one way of doing things. I take a different approach. I think the birds deserve as much freedom as I can possibly give them. I remember visiting a zoo many years ago and watching the tigers pacing restlessly up and down inside their cages. They looked so sad and bored, it broke my heart. You might argue that by keeping the ravens at the Tower at all we're restricting their freedom just like those tigers', and that's true. But then you might say the same about any animal or bird or fish or creature of any kind that's kept and cared for in any circumstances other than in the wild.

As Ravenmaster, I believe it's my job to maintain the

tradition of the ravens living at the Tower, but it's also my job to ensure that the traditions are managed in a way that's appropriate for the twenty-first century. I believe that our ravens act as ambassadors for ravens worldwide, reminding the public of the importance and role of birds in our lives. If you grant that there's a good reason to keep the birds here, then the only real question is how to do it.

So how do I keep the birds here? I certainly don't break their wings, as I once heard a visiting tour guide suggest. Nor do I pluck out their flight feathers when they're young to stop them from growing back. And I most certainly do not drug them in order to prevent them from flying. Unlikely as any of those explanations sound, I have heard even more unlikely explanations and conspiracy theories over the years: that the birds are tagged and electronically controlled, or that we have some sort of force field around the Tower. Some people even ask if the ravens are real.

If they're not, I'm out of a job.

When I became the Ravenmaster, I realized through trial and a lot of error and by following my own instincts that it was unnecessary to continue trimming the birds' primary and secondary feathers all the way back. What I do instead is trim the feathers as little as possible, depending on the size and weight of the bird and the season. In the summer I let their flight feathers grow almost to the point that they're in full flight, and then in the winter, because I like to be able to keep an eye on them throughout the dark and cold months, I trim a little more. I always trim a paired female's feathers slightly more than her male counterpart's, because I know the male will follow the female wherever she goes, so the paired males are almost always in full flight. And Merlina, because she'd been humanized—or imprinted—before she came to us, and because we've spent so many years now together, I trim very little, if at all, partly because it doesn't matter how much flight feather I trim from her, she'll always find a way of getting up onto the rooftops.

This minimum trim approach has a lot of advantages. It allows the ravens to use their wings, which keeps them healthier through exercise and the use of their flight muscles, and it gives them more of a chance of escape if they are ever attacked by a predator. It does also mean that the birds are capable of leaving the Tower—but it's a risk I am willing to take.

I judge how much I should trim from each raven by observation and intuition. If I see a raven fly from the enclosure up to around the level of the steps at the White Tower, that's about right. But if they can fly up and around the top of the Tower like a helicopter whizzing about, then I know that they might need a haircut.

The ravens' feathers only grow from about March until the end of September, so trimming takes place for each bird only a few times a year. With the aid of one of my assistants I catch the raven as gently as I possibly can, hold it to my chest, stretch out the wing and then trim a tiny amount of the feather with a pair of scissors, sometimes the primary but mostly the secondary flight feathers. An inch of feather makes all the difference. I then let them calm down and they're straight back out again.

And so far, so good. We have never lost any ravens on my watch.

Well, not quite.

11

THE GREAT ESCAPE

October 2010. Early morning. Dark, cold, but dry. An autumn day like any other. The White Tower had been covered in scaffolding for a few years, as part of a major conservation project to ensure that the ancient stonework would be around for future generations to enjoy. The whole of the western side of the Tower was wrapped in canvas and metal. The only parts of the Tower still visible were the weathervanes and the golden crowns at the top, a constant reminder that the Tower is indeed a royal palace—and that the prevailing winds in the U.K. are predominantly from the southwest.

During the work on the Tower we had to move the ravens' cages. The constant clanging of the scaffold poles and the tapping of the stonemason's mallet was likely to cause them stress, so we set up a temporary enclosure a good distance away, comprising a few old cages with some wooden sheds inside. The shed windows had all been removed, allowing access for the birds to be able to perch and shelter.

In the dawning light of this October morning I made my usual way to check on the birds.

I stopped just short of the cages to watch the birds and noticed that Munin didn't seem to be around. At first I wasn't too concerned, because she often preferred to stay inside the shed at night.

I shone my flashlight to get a better look. Bran, Munin's partner at the time, was happily perched on a branch, going through his morning routine, grooming his long black flight feathers. He looked up, stared at me menacingly for a moment and then, reassured that I was no threat, continued on. Bran was an absolute brute of a bird and hated all humans. He'd attack any visitor who happened to get in his way or who had something that he thought should have been his. Bran it was who once attacked a cameraman while I was conducting an interview for a news program. So notorious were his antics that the raven team had nicknamed him Bran the Thug, which isn't very nice, but which was perfectly accurate. (It's said that one of the ravens who worked on Alfred Hitchcock's *The Birds*—based on the story by Daphne du Maurier about a family coming under attack from all types of murderous birds—was so easygoing that he refused to attack any of the actors. Bran was the opposite. We always handled him with extreme caution, using thick leather gloves and protective glasses. Alas, he never really settled into Tower life and was finally discharged, SNLR—Service No Longer Required. Some ravens just never settle here, and rather than see them get sick or distressed, or cause problems with the other birds,

I always send them to a breeder, where they can live away from the public and the very particular demands of Tower life.)

Anyway, Bran never stirred as I unlocked the door and popped inside the shed to check if Munin was there. Indeed, to my great relief, she was—but in a flash she darted through my legs, out of the shed and out the door, which I had conspicuously failed to shut behind me! Mistake number one. Munin clearly wanted out of her temporary lodgings, and I had been well and truly ambushed. I whirled around to see Bran watching me. He was definitely in on it.

•

So I had a raven unexpectedly on the loose, which is bad enough because it can upset the other ravens' routines, but worse, as part of my minimum-trim program I hadn't trimmed Munin's feathers for several weeks, which meant she was almost in full flight . . .

Munin's powerful wings allowed her to gain height quickly and she flew higher and higher and higher into the dawning sky, until finally, majestically, she looped her way around the White Tower, as if on a victory lap, and then disappeared.

The oldest and by far the most cunning of all of our ravens, Munin has always preferred to spend her time around the Tower up as high as she can possibly get, watching the throngs of tourists below, scanning for opportunities for food theft and general mischief-making. I'm a pretty good climber—or at least I was—and have long since become accustomed to coaxing Munin down from some high defensive wall. Even today, one of her favorite games is to hide from me in the evenings when it's time to put the ravens to bed, especially when it's pouring rain, freezing cold, and I'm exhausted.

But this was different. This was clearly a full-scale breakout. I had no idea what to do. I just stood watching, mouth wide open, like some helpless chick waiting to be fed. I'd never had a raven fly off on my watch before. I needed to regain control of the situation—and fast.

I shut the cage door, ensuring all the other ravens were present, and then moved as swiftly as I could to the south side of the White Tower to see whether I could spot the escapee. Nothing. I hurriedly searched all of her normal hiding places in the hope she might have landed somewhere familiar, but to no avail. Munin had well and truly gone. I had failed in my duty. I had let down Her Majesty, the Tower, and indeed the ravens, who were all now getting restless and requiring feeding and taking care of, so I rushed through the rest of my morning routine, cleaning, feeding, chopping meat, scrubbing the water bowls, all the while hoping that Munin would miraculously appear back at the enclosure with a cheeky smile, and everything would be back to normal. It was not to be.

I knew that Munin was mischievous, but I just couldn't work out why she would want to leave the Tower, though in retrospect I suppose all the disruption with the maintenance on the White Tower must have disturbed her. Maybe she just needed to get away. Maybe she needed a break. It was all too much. We've all had that feeling.

I finished my chores, checked the sky once more in forlorn hope and resigned myself to the fact that she'd gone.

I went back to my home in the Casemates and informed the Tower control room about the loss of a raven, which was duly logged. Later during the day I informed the rest of Team Raven, the Tower's Head of Operations, the press team, and the Duty Governor. Does the Tower really crumble and the kingdom fall if the ravens leave? No, but it certainly causes a bit of a headache.

•

The Tower has lost birds before, for all sorts of reasons. An article in the *Cork Examiner* in 1896, for example, states that two ravens flew from the Tower to the dome of St. Paul's and never returned. On the night of September 13–14, 1946, meanwhile, the Tower records simply note that "Gripp the raven disappeared. He had hopped about Tower Green since April 1939 and was 17 years old." And on September 13, 1960, according to the same Tower records, Raven Grog was reported AWOL: "Last seen in the 'Rose and Punchbowl' pub in the East End of London!" A shock report in the London *Evening Standard* on August 23, 1995, "Treason at the Tower as Charlie kills raven," revealed that a police sniffer dog, a springer spaniel named Charlie, killed a raven also named Charlie during a routine security check.

(According to the report, no disciplinary action was taken against the dog.)

•

Standard operating procedure if we lose a raven is this: If one raven goes missing we replace it immediately. And if two ravens were to go missing—we would replace them immediately. But if we ever had a catastrophic loss of all of the birds—well, let's just hope that never happens.

If we do lose a bird, it's obviously very sad for me and my team. We Yeoman Warders consider the ravens to be the true guardians of the Tower, so you can imagine our distress if we're a raven down. Fortunately, though, we do like to keep one another going with a bit of good old-fashioned soldierly banter and ridicule—and on the day Munin disappeared I certainly got both barrels from my colleagues.

I couldn't get her off my mind. Where had she flown to? Which direction would she have traveled in? Would she be okay on her own? Was she even alive? Had she been attacked? Perhaps someone would realize she was a raven from the Tower of London and phone to report her. Ravens are, after all, relatively easy to spot in a crowd—they're certainly not sparrows or pigeons—and they tend to make one hell of a racket. I found myself waiting for a call with good or bad news, staring helplessly into the sky in case Munin might just appear, soaring over the Tower.

My duty for the day was guarding the inner circuit, which we Yeoman Warders patrol in rotation. I was on my last rotation, at the Bloody Tower, a job that involves looking after the safety of visitors while they queue. Once the queue had died down, I retreated to one of the little black sentry boxes provided for us well over a century ago, in case of inclement weather. As I sat miserably watching the last remaining visitors walk past, I realized that I wasn't the only one missing Munin that day. The other ravens had all been unusually quiet. I sensed that they felt her loss too.

The day was nearly over when my radio crackled into life.

"Ravenmaster Chris Skaife. Over." It was one of my colleagues, sounding rather animated.

"Send. Over."

"Chris, look on top of the gold crown on the south side of the White Tower. Is that a raven? Over."

"Roger, let me check. Wait out."

I climbed out of the sentry box and looked up at the White Tower, bandaged in its canvas and scaffolding. My eyes strained to see what looked like a small black dot right on the very tip of one of the White Tower's golden crowns. Was that her? It was impossible to tell. You get little black dots sitting up on top of the White Tower every day. It's the favorite lookout post for every crow in London, and from a distance it's difficult to distinguish a crow from a raven. It's only in flight you can tell, by the raven's distinctive diamond-shaped tail and its four long, thin flight feathers. I stood for a moment staring and listening, and then suddenly I heard it: Munin's distinctive *cr-r-ruck*-ing sound. It was her! She'd returned to the Tower. Great!

All I needed to do now was to get her down.

"Last caller, yes, it's Munin. Thank you for spotting her. Over."

"Roger, Chris. Good luck getting her down. Out."

It wasn't luck I needed. What I needed was a rope and some crampons.

The Tower was finally closed for the evening and the last remaining visitors were being shepherded out by the Yeoman Warders. I stood looking up at Munin. I wondered if she might be hungry. Maybe I should go and get a delicious mouse or a rat from the store and she would see me waving it around and would glide down, perch on my arm and gratefully take the mouse in her beak? No. That was never going to happen. This was Munin, after all. My old adversary. I had one option and one option only.

I should state clearly, before I explain what happened next, that I was not at any time asked, persuaded, or coerced by any member of Historic Royal Palaces to carry out the actions I undertook! This was my decision, foolhardy as it was. It just seemed like the right thing to do at the time for the sake of raven preservation—and, possibly, my pride.

•

Now, you might well be thinking that it's no big deal to climb the White Tower, that a former British infantry soldier with plenty of free-fall parachute experience and nearly twenty-five years of service all around the globe could easily scale the White Tower, grab a raven, and climb back down again with the bird under his arm, thus ensuring that the nation is saved. But remember: I was only in the army, I'm not James bloomin' Bond! I may at one time have been perfectly happy throwing myself out of airplanes at twelve thousand feet, but a few years on and I have to say that the prospect of climbing the White Tower and risking my life for the sake of a raven was rather daunting. I'm not quite as agile and fit as I used to be. I used to be able to run with fifty or sixty kilos on my back every day, but jumping out of airplanes and firing machine guns can leave you with a few aches and pains: my right knee is made of steel, I've got five prolapsed discs in my back, and I'm a little bit hard of hearing from all the gunfire. Plus, I've been in a few car crashes in my time. Nonetheless . . .

A complex system of scaffold poles surrounded the west side of the White Tower, supporting a series of wooden platforms allowing the stonemasons to carry out work on the ancient stone walls. There were seven or eight levels connected by ladders, not unlike a set of metal fire escapes running up the side of a building.

I checked to make sure no one was watching me and took a last glance up at the golden crown where Munin was triumphantly perched, busy preening herself. Right, I thought, I'm coming to get you, you little minx.

I climbed over a barrier and into the stonemasons' yard. Sitting on a dusty old table were two bright-yellow hard hats. I removed my precious Yeoman Warder's bonnet and tried on one of the hard hats for size, conscious that during my ascent I should try to observe at least some basic health and safety rules. But then I realized I looked utterly ridiculous in a yellow hard hat and my Yeoman Warder's uniform. I decided on the high-risk, high-style no-hat option.

I made my way to the scaffold steps and started to climb, level by level, higher and higher in a continuous spiral of metal, until I reached the very last platform on top of the roof of the White Tower. I paused to regain my breath and looked over the narrow wall at the tiny world below. I'd been up here once before, but that time I'd climbed the internal staircase, not the scaffold steps on the outside. This is pretty high, I thought.

And there she was. Munin's jet-black feathers glistened in the fading light of the evening as she rubbed her powerful beak from side to side, cleaning it on the edge of the gold crown and gazing out over London's vast glass-and-concrete horizon, as if she didn't have a care in the world. The view was certainly impressive, but I wasn't here for sightseeing. Cautiously, very cautiously, I made my way along the upper platform to the base of the turret. My heart was pounding so hard I thought I might faint. I just about squeezed my way along, my uniform snagging on the clamps that joined scaffold pole to scaffold pole. Above my head just one narrow wooden platform remained, at the very base of the weathervane. If I could just hold my nerve and get up there, then I could assess the situation and plan the capture. My uniform was by now filthy with stone dust, but it was too late to worry about keeping up appearances. Nobody could see me from here. I suddenly felt very vulnerable and alone.

I was barely twenty feet from Munin and could see through a small gap in the canvas hoarding that she was becoming sleepy as the light was fading. She must have been exhausted. It was now or never. I managed to scramble up onto the top platform. Now I had her in my direct line of sight. I was actually standing on top of the turret and its lead-lined cupola. All that was above me was the sky and the weathervane—and Munin. Below me, 150 feet away, was the cold hard earth. If I could just balance on the cupola and pull myself up toward Munin by hanging on to the weathervane with one hand, then I could perhaps get enough of a stretch to make a grab for her with the other. I had no choice but to make my move.

The moment I realized that my plan was deeply flawed was when I found myself spinning around, watching the sky above me like water disappearing into a whirlpool. I remember catching a glimpse of Munin flying off in the direction of the setting sun and somehow managing to grab hold of the weathervane—how I survived I've no idea. I had catastrophically failed to account for the simple fact that a weathervane turns on its axis according to the changing whims of the wind, and as I reached out and held it, I'd been spun around in a northeasterly direction, turning me away from Munin and missing my chance to grab her.

On my long list of bloody stupid things that I've done in my life, this one is right up there. In fact, it's only now, years later, that I can confess to this ludicrous escapade. And all for the sake of the birds.

As I always warn: Do as I say, not as I do.

The climb down the Tower was a long walk of shame. Munin had outwitted me and escaped again.

She had flown the Tower.

12

RESISTANCE TO INTERROGATION

After Munin's disappearance from the White Tower, days passed, and then the weekend came, and there were still no reports of a raven hanging around London or chilling out with the pigeons in Trafalgar Square. It would have been unheard of for a raven to return to the Tower after so many days away, so we marked her down officially as AWOL. Then I got the call—a radio message from the Tower's control room.

"Ravenmaster, over."

"Send. Over."

"We have just received a call from a Blue Badge Guide in Greenwich, stating she has seen a raven at the Royal Observatory and she wondered if we're missing one."

"How does she know it's a raven?"

"She said it's very large and wearing a dark green leg band."

Munin!

"Is the bird still there?"

"Yep. Up a tree in Greenwich Park."

"Thank you, control room. I'm on my way. Roger, out."

I had a chance to redeem myself after my weathervane antics. This time Munin would not escape.

But of course she did.

My assistant Shady and I raced—okay, drove just about within the limits of the law—to Greenwich. Munin was up a tree right next to one of the Observatories, causing quite a commotion with the visitors and staff, croaking and cronking as loudly as she could and generally making one hell of a racket. Shady and I thought about climbing the tree, but it was big, wet, and slippery from all the rain, and we were perhaps a little past our best tree-climbing days. Besides, when we approached, Munin simply hopped higher and higher, from branch to branch. There was nothing we could do. We were Yeoman Warders—we were hardly going to call the fire brigade to help us catch a bird. We had no choice but to retreat to the Tower and come up with a Plan B.

I returned to Greenwich Park the following morning on the pretense of walking my dogs. I didn't want to draw unnecessary attention to myself, so I left my uniform behind. I stopped at very nearly every tree in the park, hour after hour, hoping Munin would still be around somewhere. I figured she was hungry by now, so I carefully examined all the park's bins and all the cafés and the ice cream parlors and the entrance to the Royal Observatory, which was crowded with tourists milling around, just the sort of place I know Munin likes to target. But in the end, I gave up again and returned to the Tower thoroughly dejected. In Munin I had truly met my match.

Ravens will do whatever it takes to survive. This explains their reputation for cruelty: They will feed on carrion and carcasses. They will live anywhere, in any conditions. They are prepared to push themselves and others to the limit to get what they want. You've got to admire that.

I can remember during my time in the army I was asked if I wanted to go on a specialist survival course. I was up for anything, so I said yes and I asked one of my mates if he wanted to come with me. What sort of survival course is it, he asked, mushroom picking up in Scotland? That's about right, I said, mushroom picking up in Scotland. And so he signed up as well.

It turned out the course was a long-range reconnaissance and resistance to interrogation course with Special Forces in Germany. There just happened to be a couple of spare places for anyone foolish enough to volunteer. Me and my mate were pretty fit infantry soldiers with plenty of experience in the military behind us by then, but this was something else: escape and evasion, being hunted by dogs and a hunter force, and then the inevitable capture and interrogation.

It was what you might call an interesting experience. I won't go into all the details, but suffice it to say that there are all sorts of techniques that are used during interrogation training to try to extract information from you and you're only supposed to offer up the big five: name, rank, number, date of birth, and blood group. You're sleep-deprived and then bombarded with all sorts of questions and scenarios to try to get you to talk. To my surprise, on one of the tests—it was a recall and memory test—I found I had no trouble resisting interrogation. I managed to stay awake as my interrogator banged on for two hours and I was able to recall everything he had to say. You were supposed to fall asleep exhausted, but I rather enjoyed listening to him. "I'll say this for you, Chris," the instructor said at the end of the course, "you are one of the most boring gits I've ever met in my life." On the way back home I remember my mate turning to me and saying, "Well, that wasn't mushroom picking in Scotland, Chris, was it."

Dealing with Munin is not mushroom picking in Scotland.

•

A few days after her escape to Greenwich, I received yet another call from the Tower's control room.

Apparently, a gentleman who lived near Greenwich Park was claiming he'd caught a raven and was currently holding it under house arrest—in a sports bag! Incredibly, armed only with the bag and a blanket, a thick pair of garden gloves, and some chicken legs, he'd managed to capture Munin, which is certainly more than I'd managed with all my years of experience.

Shady and I once again raced down to Greenwich. I knocked on the gentleman's front door.

"I think I may have one of your ravens in my kitchen," he said.

"I believe you have, sir, and we would very much like her back."

We were duly escorted into his kitchen, and lo and behold, there she was, the escapee happily secured in a sports bag, with her head poking out and her beady little eyes looking inquisitively around the room. We placed her into her travel box, thanked the gentleman for his great act of kindness and for helping us to save the kingdom, and made our way back to the Tower.

The following day Munin was no worse for her travels, although she was a little underweight, so I decided to keep her safe in the enclosure for a few weeks in order to monitor her health and get her back to her regular size. I thought it might also give her time to reflect on her actions. Me too: Munin's great escape taught me a very simple lesson, one that over the course of my career as Ravenmaster I have had to learn again and again. And again.

Never ever underestimate the ravens.

13

CITIZENS OF
THE WORLD

Ravens may sometimes be hard to spot, but they can be found everywhere. The editors of the most authoritative guide to European birds, *Birds of the Western Palearctic*—or to give it its full title, *Handbook of the Birds of Europe, the Middle East, and North Africa: The Birds of the Western Palearctic*, nine volumes, not exactly light reading—write that for the raven the concept of habitat is "so wide-ranging that the concept of habitat is hardly applicable," which is a good way of putting it. Ravens are cosmopolitan creatures, so it might be easier to state where they're *not* at home than where they are. You won't find them, apparently, in Novaya Zemlya, which is that little archipelago in the Arctic right up at the north of Russia and Europe, or indeed in parts of Siberia. But otherwise, where there are deserts, mountains, moors, forests, cliffs, coasts, towns, villages, or cities, you will find ravens or one of their subspecies.

Corvus corax hispanus: Iberia, Balearic Islands, Sardinia.

Corvus corax laurencei: from the eastern Mediterranean through the Middle East and all the way to China. *Corvus corax tingitanus*: north African coastal regions. *Corvus corax canariensis*: the Canary Islands. *Corvus corax varius*: Faeroes and Iceland. *Corvus corax kamtschaticus*: Mongolia and Japan. *Corvus corax tibetanus*: have a guess. *Corvus corax sinuatus*: western North America and Central America. And of course, *Corvus corax principalis*, known as the common or northern raven in North America. They get everywhere. In 1921, according to Bannerman's *Birds of the British Isles*, ravens were even found scavenging at the British Mount Everest expedition at a height of 21,000 feet!

For all their ubiquity, these days the Tower of London is one of the few places a visitor to the U.K. is likely to see a raven—unless you're visiting the Welsh hills or the Scottish Highlands, or the uplands of northern England. According to Derek Ratcliffe, in his great book—*the* definitive book on ravens—*The Raven: A Natural History in Britain and Ireland*, "Although abundant in London in 1500, the Raven was almost gone by 1800." What happened?

During the eighteenth and nineteenth centuries, ravens came to be regarded as pests who spread disease, as enemies of the farmer and the shepherd with his flock, and as vermin in the towns and cities, and they were hunted almost to the point of extinction. They were hated and feared. Bounties were placed upon their heads, their nests destroyed. Indeed, it wasn't until 1981 that ravens in the U.K. were protected under the Wildlife and Countryside Act—before that, they were fair game. Fortunately, numbers have increased: according to the Royal Society for the Protection of Birds, there are currently seventy-four hundred breeding pairs in the U.K. and Ireland, though this is still a tiny number compared to estimates of, say, a million crows and half a million magpies. It takes a long time for a species to recover from persecution.

There is no doubt that ravens in the wild can be pests, especially juvenile ravens when they gather together in great numbers. Yet for all their unpopularity, they remain strongly associated with the glories of Britain's ancient past, their symbolic role in British life and culture far exceeding and outlasting their actual presence in our lives. There was a poet, John Clare, one of the great working-class poets of England, a peasant poet who often bemoaned the destruction of the countryside and who wrote a lot about birds. In his poem "The Raven's Nest" he imagines a world unchanging, where the ravens return each year to the village, "where still they live, / Through changes winds and storms and are secure / And like a landmark in the chronicles / Of village memorys treasured up yet lives / The huge old oak that wears the raven's nest." Nice that, isn't it, the idea of the raven and its nest storing up the village memory? Ravens not as omens of ill but as dark recording angels.

The raven is indeed so closely identified with the British countryside that it has kindly lent its name to dozens of villages, towns, rivers, fields, farms, and homesteads. In Cumbria, for example, you have a Raven Beck, several Raven Crags and a Ravencragg. In Scotland there's a Raven Craig. There's also a Ravensdale (in Yorkshire), an East Ravendale (in Lincolnshire), Ravenfield (again in Yorkshire), a couple of Ravenheads (in Cheshire and Merseyside), more Raven Hills than you could count, plus Raven Rocks, Raven Scars, Ravenstones, Ravensides and Ravenswoods. In Scotland, you have your Corbiewell and Corby Loch. Ravens are written into the landscape.

And written in the skies as well. There is a small constellation of stars in the Southern Hemisphere called Corvus, which roughly resembles the raven, and which was so named by the second-century astronomer Ptolemy, based on a strange story about the god Apollo, who sent a raven to fetch some water. The raven took a bowl for the water and flew off, but then spotted some figs. He tasted the figs, but they weren't ripe, and so he waited until they were. He then flew back to Apollo with a water snake and lied to him, saying the snake had blocked the stream where he had gone to fetch water, which is why it had taken him so long. But Apollo knew exactly what the raven was up to and condemned him and his kind to be able to drink no water until figs are ripened, which is apparently why ravens sound so parched! He threw the raven, the bowl and the snake into the zodiac, and now the four brightest stars, Gamma, Delta, Epsilon, and Beta Corvi, form the constellation Corvus. It's one of the great raven stories.

One day when I'm retired I might go and visit all the different raven towns and villages in Britain and Ireland and all the raven-associated places and species around the world, gathering up all the incredible myths and stories. I know there's a Raven's Brew coffee company over in Ketchikan in Alaska: they claim their coffee is "The Last Legal High." That'd be a fun trip. And the Baltimore Ravens of course, the American football team. I also rather fancy visiting the ravens of Australia: *Corvus coronoides*, *Corvus mellori*, and *Corvus tasmanicus*, which is rapidly disappearing. I've been lucky enough to spot ravens in the wild in a few places on my travels over the years. In Cornwall, I once spotted two specks against a patch of blue sky amongst dark gray drifting clouds, circling side by side, wing tip to wing tip. They were diving and turning in formation and then ascending in circles again. I can still see it now: the ravens dancing in flight like that moved me more than any human performance ever could.

I just wish I'd been paying rather more attention to the wildlife all those years ago when I was in the army. Who knows what I missed. I remember sometimes we'd be out on patrol in Northern Ireland, in South Armagh, and I'd stop the team and signal them to go to ground because there was some vole or field mouse by the side of the road, or a hare or a rabbit prancing across the fields. The other soldiers thought I was crazy. But it made a nice change from looking out for IRA snipers.

In fact, I remember after our first tour in Northern Ireland, we briefly returned back to the battalion base before being deployed on a six-month unaccompanied tour in Belize. Belize! If only I'd been paying attention in Belize!

We prepared for the Belize tour in the traditional British

Army fashion, by doing some jungle training—in the winter, in the snow, in Thetford in Norfolk. I'd certainly never been anywhere like Belize before. Formerly British Honduras, the country had just been granted independence when we got there, but there were still British soldiers garrisoned as a deterrent force. The place was like a dream. This was where I first took up scuba diving, diving off the coral reefs, with the barracudas and the hammerhead sharks: an underwater world I'd never imagined. And the sheer range of natural habitats: over half of Belize is forest, where you get these wild pigs and deer and these creatures called tapirs, thick-set little creatures which look like black pigs with long snouts, and which are nocturnal and feed on fruit and you'd follow their tracks through the jungle to find water holes and you'd find them there swimming, their snouts up in the air like snorkels. I loved the little tapirs. And then you've got your howler monkeys up in the trees, and your crocodiles in the rivers, the jaguars, the pumas. And snakes. Lots and lots of snakes. And spiders.

Though I didn't realize it at the time, Belize is a birdwatcher's paradise. If only I could get back to Belize now, knowing everything I know about birds! I'd go and look at the keel-billed toucan, and the collared aracari, and the blue-crowned motmot, the slaty-tailed trogon, the jabiru, the boat-billed heron, snail kites, American pygmy kingfishers—the list of incredible birds in Belize goes on and on.

As it was, I was too busy surviving in the jungle to take much notice of the bird life. I loved Belize. Being in Belize was a bit like being a kid in Dover, having to survive out in the wild, building A-frames, making fires, learning tracking and trapping skills. It suited me really well. The only thing that was different was the sound of the jungle at night—this constant humming and buzzing. Popping sounds and grunts and screeches. The never-ending sound of the jungle. And not just never-ending, the sheer volume of it. Sometimes, if you were driving down a track, the sound of the locusts and the crickets would be so loud it would drown out the sound of the Land Rover. We'd be rattling along and there'd be wild turkeys or pigs and the section commander would take a potshot, in case he could bag something for our tea. It was wild.

•

Belize may have been a missed opportunity for me as a bird-watcher, but then how many of us can honestly say we bother to pay attention to the birds and animals around us every day? Until I started working with the ravens I might have called myself an animal lover, but really I had no clue about animal behavior or animal intelligence, let alone all the great folklore and stories and symbols associated with animals. I just took them for granted. Growing up, we had a tortoise, we had rabbits, we had cats named Ginny, Whisky, and Sherry—spot the connection?—and dogs, including a Jack Russell called Ringo who bit me so badly he was taken away, and Bess the basset hound, who sadly died after I'd taken her on a *very* long walk. When we were posted to Cyprus my wife and I lived in a house in Limassol with a big garden and we ended up with a collection of twenty-two stray cats! They were everywhere in Cyprus and we'd take them in, look after them, and get them neutered at the vet. I remember one cat giving birth to her kittens one night on our bed, in fact. But for me it's not the cats or the dogs, it's the ravens who have taught me everything I know about the complexities of human and nonhuman animal relationships.

14

DOUBLE-HATTING

Once I've released the ravens from the enclosure in the morning I nip back to my house in the Casemates, give my dogs a quick walk in the moat, get changed into my uniform, and it's time to get on with the day job.

I've always been what you might call a double-hatter. In the army, I was a specialist machine gunner. I'll never forget the first time I fired a submachine gun on a 25-meter range. It was a completely useless old thing, really, and wouldn't have shot through a wet paper bag, but I thought it was brilliant. The sound of it, the smell of it—cordite and gun oil. I just loved it. And the old SLRs, of course, the self-loading rifles, they had a real kick to them: it was like firing an elephant gun. Because I'm left-handed I had to learn everything round the other way, but nothing could dim my enthusiasm. I specialized in SF—sustained fire. You've got your general-purpose machine gun, your GPMG, 7.62mm round, set up on a tripod, with a C2 sight, which allows you to fire out to ranges greater than 1,100 meters, and you work in a two-man team in your platoon to provide fire support. With a GPMG and a sight you can fire over hills! You can imagine the adrenaline at night in a platoon with nine guns in your team.

As well as being a gunner I was also a drummer, which was as much a surprise to me as to anyone else. For me, playing music was an acquired rather than an innate skill—and certainly not a skill I was ever planning to acquire. I can remember on our very first day when I joined up, we were all lined up in an old aircraft hangar and our Platoon Commander came out and told us that we were going to be drummers. You'll be infantry soldiers, he said, but you'll also learn how to play the drum and fife. We couldn't believe it! You can imagine what we said. We were youngsters—sixteen-, seventeen-year-olds, kids really—and we'd joined up to be "proper" soldiers. We thought we'd be out in the Falklands or somewhere, just like that. We didn't realize we were going to have to spend eighteen months before we were assigned to our regiments learning to play the drum and fife! So we rebelled against it. Somebody got a petition going and we presented it the next day to the Platoon Commander and it wasn't long before we were all lined up in the aircraft hangar and this old Drum Major came out of his office with his parade stick, waving it around, telling us we were all going to be shot for treachery. I was genuinely scared.

We weren't shot for treachery.

Instead, over the next eighteen months, to my surprise, I became a part of a Corps of Drums as well as an infantryman—and I absolutely loved it. To this day the British Army still maintains a Corps of Drums in most infantry battalions. It's an important part of the ceremony and rituals of military life.

Drummers are a little bit different. We think differently. We behave differently. It's often the case that if there's someone in a platoon and they're not fitting in, they're put into the Corps of Drums, because drummers are always seen as a bit, shall we say, unusual. A little bit independent-minded, a little bit quirky. The training for a drummer is also different. As junior soldiers, in the mornings we'd be out digging trenches or bayonet training and then we'd have music lessons in the afternoons. Most of us had never had a music lesson in our lives, and the ones we got in the army were certainly not like what you might have had at school. The section corporal would come out and he'd say, "This is the note G," and he'd show you how to play the note G on your fife and he had a big bass drumstick and if you played the wrong note he'd just bang you on the head with it. And that's how I learned how to play music—being banged on the head for eighteen months with a bass drumstick by a section corporal! It seemed to work: we formed a nice little Corps of Drums, and many years later I eventually became a Drum Major myself.

(And just to be *absolutely* clear, for the record, since even some of my friends and family—and occasionally even a Yeoman Warder—tend to get confused about this, or like to pretend they're confused: drummers are not bandsmen. Bandsmen play musical instruments primarily for entertainment and delight: they are musicians. Drummers do not play primarily for entertainment and delight, as you'll know if you've ever heard a Corps of Drums going at it full pelt. Drummers are fully trained infantry soldiers who also happen to play the drums.)

As an infantry drummer you have to prove yourself twice over. As you progress in your career you have to do twice the number of courses and take on twice the responsibility. Which was always fine by me. It also means that caring for the ravens in addition to my other work as a Yeoman Warder has never been a problem. For some people it might be a bit of a hassle. For me, I couldn't imagine my life here without them. I don't so much look at it as having two jobs as having twice as much fun. Part of the fun of being a Drum Major back in the day was all the dressing up for ceremonial occasions—and again, it turns out that my time in the army was preparing me for my life at the Tower.

The uniform we Yeoman Warders wear on a daily basis is what's called Blue Undress. It's not the full ceremonial uniform with the frilly Tudor ruff and the tights that you might have seen us wearing at important state occasions. (The tights used to be stockings—and the fiddle with stockings! Ladies, I had no idea.) The Blue Undress uniform consists of a tabard in royal blue and scarlet with the Queen's insignia on the front, trousers with a red stripe, a bonnet, black shoes and socks, and a big brass-buckled belt. In the winter we also have a cape. I wear the Ravenmaster's badge of office on the sleeve of my tabard, on my right arm between my wrist and my elbow. It features a raven's head, representing Brân the Blessed; the Crown, representing royalty; and a laurel wreath, which symbolizes authority. The badge of office was first worn in 1969 by the first officially appointed Ravenmaster, John Wilmington. (If you look closely you'll see slight differences in other Yeoman Warders' uniforms: some of us wear our regimental badges on our radio pouches, or regimental buttons rather than the usual standard-issue buttons.) I should probably also explain that the Queen's insignia, the big EIIR on the chest of our tabards, stands for Elizabeth II Regina. You'd be amazed at how many people ask what it means—the traditional Yeoman Warder response to such a question being something like "Extremely romantic, sir" or "Exit second right, madam." I've also heard Yeoman Warders use "Early riser," "Elderly retainer," and, of course, "Emergency Response, how can I help you?"

The Yeoman Warder's uniform—we don't call it a costume, thank you, because it is *not* a costume, it is a uniform; there is a difference: a costume is a style, a uniform is a means of identification—was designed in the mid-1800s as a more comfortable form of dress for the Warders, who before that had to wear the full ceremonial outfit every day. These days we only wear the full state uniform on special occasions or in the presence of Her Majesty the Queen. Keeping the full state uniform fresh and stiff is a task in and of itself. (That famous Tudor ruff, for example, is made of a stiffly starched white cotton, crimped together, and held in place with some pretty heavy-duty thread. It's designed to keep your neck straight and your head up in the presence of royalty, which it most certainly does.) We also have a semi-state uniform, which is basically a watered-down version of the full state. Semi-state consists of the State Dress jacket of royal scarlet, decorated with seventy-one meters of gold braid sewn onto strips of black velvet. Embroidered onto the chest is the royal crown and royal insignia and embroidered on the back is the Tudor rose of England and a thistle and shamrock, representing Scotland and Northern Ireland. In semi-state you wear white gloves and blue undress trousers but not the full state scarlet breeches, which are held tight just below the knee with gold braid and a brass buckle, adorned with Tudor rose rosettes made of red, white, and blue ribbons. Full state also requires the special highly polished shoes, with Tudor rose rosettes attached that match the rosettes on the breeches, and the dreaded scarlet woolen stockings, which are nowadays the much more practical thick tights, especially made for men with a hole at the front, for obvious purposes. (A long-standing joke is to instruct any new and unsuspecting male Yeoman Warder that the hole has to go at the rear.)

Uniform on—and it's out to meet the public.

15

THE STORY

In the Tower we organize ourselves according to an ancient system of work called the Waite, which is basically a kind of rota which ensures that there are always the right number of people on duty at the various posts throughout the Tower, day and night. There are posts on the inner circuit and posts on the outer circuit. We also work what we call Specials, which are the world-famous Yeoman Warder guided tours. Each tour lasts for about an hour, and we do three tours a day.

Doing the tours takes some getting used to. Being a Yeoman Warder requires a unique skill set, which the military doesn't entirely prepare you for: it's sort of a cross between being a security guard, a ceremonial guard, an amateur historian, and a stand-up comedian. One piece of advice: do not, *under any circumstances*, heckle a Yeoman Warder giving you a tour. All I'll say is if you come on a tour and want to heckle, it pays to have a good sense of humor and a pretty thick skin.

•

I love doing the tours. For me it's one of the best parts of the job. My tour usually begins with the words "Good morning, ladies and gentlemen, and welcome to Her Majesty's Royal Palace and Fortress, the Tower of London. My name is Chris, I'm the Ravenmaster here, and for the next five hours I'm going to be your guide . . ." The tour doesn't actually last for five hours, of course, but like all of us Yeoman Warders I could probably talk about it for at least that long, if not much longer.

When you're first taken on at the Tower you're appointed one of the older Yeoman Warders as a mentor. My mentor, now long since retired, was a brilliant tour guide, one of the greats. With your mentor you learn what we call the Story. The Story is a script about the history of the Tower and all its buildings, all of the historical events and characters connected to the Tower, all the dates and anniversaries, the ghost stories, and the stories about torture and execution and murder and mystery. It covers absolutely everything Tower-related that you can possibly think of, and you have to learn all thirteen thousand words of it. Many of the details haven't changed for more than two hundred years, since we first started admitting large numbers of visitors to the Tower in the early nineteenth century. It takes about an hour or an hour and a half to recite the whole thing, and you have to be able to recite it to your mentor verbatim, from memory, word for word, from beginning to end. The Story forms the basis of the tours—and it *is* a story. I always say to our visitors, if you want to know the actual history of the Tower, don't ask a Yeoman Warder, go and read a book. If you want to know about history, read some history. If you want to hear a story, come on a tour.

Once you've learned the Story you can improvise around it, adding your own insights and details, but not until you've learned it exactly, precisely, by heart. This way, at any time during a tour another Yeoman Warder can take over if necessary, because frankly sometimes it is necessary. Sometimes you have people who are taken ill on the tour, and there are all sorts of other problems that can arise when you're dealing with the public. You can imagine. We've seen it all. We quite often have fainters, for example, who get overcome when we talk about some of the more gruesome parts of the Tower's history.

To be a good Yeoman Warder you've got to be able to tell a good story. You've got to be a storyteller. You have to be able to captivate an audience, whether they're age eight or they're eighty, whether there's twenty of them or two hundred of them, wherever they're from, and even if English isn't their first language. It's a form of public theater, an open-air one-man or one-woman show, and your only instrument is your voice. I always warm up with a few vocal exercises— do-re-mi and a bit of *mmm*-ing and *ee*-ing for resonance— and then I'll make my way down to the Byward Tower, have a quick sip of water, and walk out to meet the group. Breathe. Smile. Talk.

You always know straightaway, within the first couple of minutes, whether you've got a good audience, and if they're a good audience, they get a great tour. And if they're not, well, they still get a great tour, but it definitely takes that extra little bit of work. You have to work the crowd. And they certainly work you. People pay a lot of money to come into the Tower, and quite rightly they want to hear the tales and legends told properly, whatever sort of a day you've had, and whatever sort of a day they're having. Sometimes you get couples who are arguing, or you get children who don't want to be there, or adults who don't want to be there, but still you've got to find a way of telling them about the two boy princes, and the Duke of Monmouth with his head sewn back on his body, and Anne Boleyn, with her lips and eyes moving after she'd been beheaded. You can't mess it up and you can't let them down. You have to find a way of telling the same stories and answering the same questions day in, day out. You not only have to find your own way of telling the Story, you also have to find your own way of retelling the Story. When I act as a mentor to Yeoman Warder trainees I always remind them that even though they might have told the story a thousand times, for the paying visitor it's their first time.

Doing a really great tour is like being a jazz musician: a moment's improvisation based on a lifetime's experience. You can learn the Story in about six months. But there's a world of difference between mere rote learning and real mastery. You can use all sorts of tricks to be able to recall the basic facts: picture association, memory palaces. My mentor taught

me all that. But to make the Story your own probably takes
three or four years of solid practice. If you're someone who
wants to tell the Story with a bit of humor, you have to learn
how to tell a joke. You have to get your timing exactly right.
You have to know what to leave out, and when to pause, what
to emphasize. And if you want to add details or facts they've
got to be accurate. There has to be a satisfying shape to
the story. And you have to have stamina. After more than
a decade of treading the boards at the Tower I'm probably as
good at it now as I'm ever going to be, but I'm still always
trying to perfect the Story.

Exactly where I get my interest in storytelling I don't
really know. At the hair salon back in Dover where my mum
and my nan worked, there was certainly a lot of chat, and my
nan Marie was also an amateur opera singer. She was a tiny
lady with a big personality, and she and my granddad were
leading lights in the Dover Operatic Society, so there was definitely something theatrical about them. They used to take
us on holiday in their beautiful old golden Humber car, with
us children rolling around in the back on the red leather
seats, and we would drive all the way to Bibione in northern
Italy, with its beautiful beach. We'd go to their house in
Dover for Christmas, and there might be up to about twenty
of us gathered around the giant table in the dining room, the
good room, and they would grind their own coffee and they
would serve us children cider and biscuits. There was a river
at the end of the garden, and we'd all head down there with
fishing nets to catch sticklebacks. We'd ride around on our

bikes and trikes. It was really a magical place. Maybe that's where I inherited my love of spectacle and theater.

Or maybe it's just human nature, to want to entertain others and ourselves. I remember back in Dover, camping out with my mates on Sugar Loaf Hill, scaring ourselves sense-less with ghost stories. I was always in the plays at school—the bright lights, the experience of putting on a show. Dressing up, the roar of the greasepaint, the smell of the crowd, all of that. I was also in the church choir. For a brief period, I was head choirboy—don't tell my Yeoman Warder colleagues, though, or I'll never hear the last of it! At school I always loved history classes because history meant stories. Real "sceptr'd isle" sort of stuff. And in the army, there were all the long nights standing guard, telling stories about old girlfriends and drunken nights on the town and tall tales from our operational tours of duty.

When I was coming toward the end of my military career I went to the army careers office to talk to them about my options and I said I might like to do something connected with history. I wouldn't say they laughed out loud, but cer-tainly their ideas about what old soldiers could do and my ideas about what I wanted to do were not the same. I knew that I wanted to do something that stretched me a bit. Un-fortunately, there are not a lot of options for history-loving storytelling infantry soldiers, let alone infantry soldiers who are drum- and fife-playing specialist machine gunners— these are *very* niche skills. Despite all of the skills I'd learned, I realized I was going to have to start all over again.

So I decided to take matters into my own hands, and while I was still serving, I took myself off to do a part-time degree course in archaeology at Sussex University. I wanted to go all the way back and start at the very beginning—I think I rather fancied myself as the next Indiana Jones. And it was great fun, let me tell you, going to university. I'd never experienced anything quite like that before: it was more of a culture shock than joining the army. Little did I know that just like my military training, all this new experience— learning how to independently research a subject, explaining your thinking in seminars and small groups—was going to put me in good stead for working at the Tower.

I was at this time on a posting down in Brighton as a PSI—a permanent staff instructor—of a machine gun platoon, training Territorials, the U.K.'s volunteer army reserve force. It was a great job. It meant I could be at home with my family much more. It was the closest thing to a normal life during my whole career in the military. This was when I started working on my degree. One day I was talking to the old caretaker at the Brighton Territorial Army Centre about my love of history and he suggested that if I liked history so much, I should apply to become a Yeoman Warder. I barely knew what a Yeoman Warder was, and I certainly didn't know you could apply to become one. He had a friend who worked up in the Jewel House at the Tower and he got me a number to ring. So I just called up the Chief Yeoman Warder and asked for an application form. Easy.

16

APPLICATION

Not so easy. I was about to apply to the Tower when I realized I didn't meet the essential criteria. I had the minimum required twenty-two years of unblemished service in the military, but you're supposed to be at least the rank of a Warrant Officer, which I was not. I was a Colour Sergeant. If you're a drummer, a Colour Sergeant is about as far as you can go, because you spend a lot of your time training and organizing the drum corps. A Colour Sergeant is just above a Sergeant but below a Warrant Officer. So it looked like I was out even before I tried to get in. Nonetheless, my wife encouraged me to apply. She's like me—she has what you might call a can-do attitude, only more so. Quite literally I wouldn't be here without her.

The Tower received about a hundred applications the year I applied—2005—and just twelve people were invited for interview. I was among them. For the interview you had to give a twenty-minute presentation on a figure from history.

I chose Henry VI, allegedly stabbed to death while at prayer in the Tower, in the Wakefield Tower, on the night of May 21, 1471. This was me, remember, who'd barely scraped through school! I did all my research—I read all the books and the articles—and I knew my presentation by heart. Instead of doing weapons training or drill with my platoon in Brighton I would get them to listen to me practicing my presentation. Brighton TA 3PWRR Machine Gun Platoon: sorry, lads.

So on the day of the interview my wife and I traveled up to the Tower. I've only ever had two job interviews, and on both occasions I was fully accompanied by the women in my life: my mum came with me to the army recruiting office in Dover back in the early 1980s, and my wife came with me to the Tower of London almost twenty-five years later!

When we arrived at the Tower, my wife went on a tour to show partners of the applicants an idea of what it might be like to live here, while those of us who'd applied for the job were gathered together to meet the Chief Yeoman Warder, who introduced himself and then organized us into groups to do our presentations. When it came to my turn I was pretty nervous, but I gave it my all and thought it went okay—except I do remember the Chief Yeoman Warder and the other Tower staff sitting there stony-faced throughout. Then we were interviewed individually. There were the standard interview questions: Why do you want to come and work here? What skills and experience can you bring to the job? Tell us about a time when you had to act as part of a team. The usual sort of thing. Then there were a few questions specific to the Tower:

How would you feel about people taking photographs of you all day long? Fortunately I'd rehearsed answers to all the questions I could anticipate. I can honestly say I put my heart and soul into that interview.

The next day I got the phone call. I didn't get the job. They'd filled the vacancy with someone else, but they said they'd put me on the waiting list. I was absolutely devastated. Having done all that work and having been to the Tower and seen the life of the Yeoman Warders, I had set my heart on becoming a part of it. I wondered if it was because I was a Colour Sergeant and not a Warrant Officer. I didn't dare ask.

I had just six months left in the army and then I was out—with no prospect of getting another job, let alone a different career. My wife and I started making other plans. But then, in one of those amazing and unexpected twists of fate that sets you off on an entirely new course in life, the Tower rang me up a couple of weeks later and said that a vacancy had unexpectedly come up. So I went back up to London and met the Governor and the head of Marketing and Visitor Services and I had to do my presentation all over again—except this time I did it even better. This was Laurence Olivier–level stuff! I was interviewed again, and they asked me why they should offer me the job. Fortunately, I'd had the presence of mind to bring with me my most recent confidential report—you get a confidential report every year in the military, and your OC writes some comments about your performance. It's famously printed on yellow paper. My OC had given me a glowing report. And so I just handed over my yellow piece of paper and said, "That's why you should offer me the job."

And the next day, July 7, 2005, they rang to offer me the job. It was the day of the London bombings, 7/7. Fifty-two people killed. Seven hundred injured. The U.K.'s first big suicide attack. That gave me a moment's pause. After twenty years of worry with me away in the army, did I really want to take my family from our safe and secure life down in Brighton to the uncertainty of a job in the very heart of London? I thought about it for about a second before saying yes.

On September 19, 2005, I left the military and became a Yeoman Warder of Her Majesty's Royal Palace and Fortress, The Tower of London, and a member of the Queen's Body Guard of the Yeoman Guard Extraordinary, responsible for security at the Tower of London and the protection of the Crown Jewels and royal regalia. For the first time in my life as an adult I was a civilian. I was sixteen when I joined the army. I was forty when I left. It was a very scary moment. When you leave the military, you have to go around with a form and get everything signed out. Your uniform goes to the Quartermaster, you get signed out from the Dental and Medical Centres. You go to your Officer Commanding, to the Company Sergeant Major, until you've seen everybody, and you're left with nothing. You suddenly go from being a part of a family to being on your own. For those of you who have not had the experience, imagine retiring not just from your job, but from your entire life: you lose your home, your friends, your support network. A lot of ex-soldiers find they can't cope.

They end up drinking. Their marriages break down. Some of us end up on the streets. It's pretty tough. I was one of the lucky ones. The Tower and the ravens have been my salvation.

I used to think the old Ravenmasters were a bit weird when they talked about the birds all the time: they just seemed so wrapped up in it all. It was as if nothing else mattered to them. But now I understand. They're my life. If you're doing the job right, it's all-consuming. It's about always paying attention, always being alert and mindful. With the ravens out and about among the public and their fellow corvids every day you have to be vigilant, for everyone's sake. You have to be prepared. Unfortunately, we have had incidents in the past where visitors have harmed the birds, and sometimes the birds have harmed each other. Ravens are territorial creatures, and they've been known to fight to the death in territorial disputes. According to the Tower records, on May 3, 1946, for example, "As the result of an attack made by the other two Ravens, Pauline the Raven died [. . .] She had been a resident in the Tower since 12th July 1940 when she was 4 years old." And again, on October 15, 1959, "As the result of an attack by other Ravens of the Tower, GUNN died of its injuries."

I'm proud to say that on my watch no ravens have ever harmed each other—which I like to think is due to careful observation, planning, and husbandry. Ravens are creatures of habit, and even the slightest change to their daily routine can lead to stress and psychological problems. Sometimes by the time I pick up on a dispute between ravens, it's too late. Like a lot of us, they tend to hide their sicknesses and their grievances. I assume it's a self-protection mechanism. I'm not an expert on raven social systems, but I can see that they have complex social lives, with feuds and disagreements between them, just as we humans do. One important sign of stress or illness or problems among them is a decrease in weight, so I weigh them at least once a month and keep a detailed log. A weak raven can quickly become vulnerable and can get picked on by the others. Especially around the early part of the year, after the breeding season, when the adult ravens reestablish their territorial positions around the Tower, things can get a little bit lively. But that's exactly why I enjoy caring for the birds. I see it as my job to make sure they're safe here—safe from one another and from all other threats. Sometimes a quick decision can save a raven's life and protect the public. At other times, it's just the day in, day out discharge of your duties that matters: your focus and commitment to keeping the system greased and clean and in good working order, keeping the show on the road.

I used to think that my military career came to an end when I left the army, but now I see that it was merely my apprenticeship.

17

SPEAKING IN RAVENISH

Yes, I talk to the ravens. And yes, they talk to me.

Or at least, I imitate them, and they imitate me.

I'm not exactly Doctor Dolittle, but I suppose I have developed a way of communicating with them over the years that seems to work for us all. I always say "Good morning" to them. And "Good night." And I speak to them—in English—during the day. I've also developed a few raven calls and sounds, which they seem to respond to, though I don't exactly know how—birdsong and bird communication are such complex things and I can't pretend to fully understand it. People spend their whole lives studying birdsong. I'm merely a practitioner.

Here's what I do know. The name of the raven, *Corvus corax*, comes from the Greek *korax*, meaning a croaker, but ravens in fact make a much deeper sound than the more familiar sound of a crow's croaking, which sounds like "caw-caw" and which sort of rattles and clicks. That's not the sound of a raven at all. A raven's call sounds hoarse, but when you listen to it carefully, it's also rather resonant—and commanding. It carries with it an authority that is entirely lacking in your common or garden crow's croak. The Bella Bella Indians, the Heiltsuk, the indigenous people of British Columbia, revered the raven in their culture, calling him "The One Whose Voice Is to Be Obeyed." If not to be obeyed, it's certainly a voice to be listened to. Comparing it to a crow's call I'd describe it as more of a "cronk" than a "caw." I've read many studies in which raven calls are variously described as "pruk," "kruk," "quork," "kaah," "krrk," "nuk," "tok," "cr-r-ruck," "kwulkulkul," and, for some reason, "wonk-wonk," but perhaps Dickens comes closest when he describes a raven's voice as a sound "not unlike the drawing of some eight or ten dozen of long corks." Exactly! It's the sound of the drawing of corks. Maybe that's why I love it. Some of the latest research suggests that there are eighty distinct raven calls, with regional dialects and variations. I could probably identify a dozen or so calls from our birds.

Learning basic raven, what I refer to as Ravenish, involves becoming familiar with the pitch and length of the birds' calls. Of course, each bird sounds different, though fortunately a lot of the communication is perfectly obvious: they're often calling out in defense of their territory, for example, or in a general call of challenge. It's also common for ravens to mimic other birds and all sorts of other sounds: car alarms, road traffic signals. In the stories and legends of the indigenous people of the Pacific Northwest Coast—the Tlingit, the

Haida, the Tsimshian, the Heiltsuk, the Miwok, and many others—the raven often features as a kind of trickster figure who takes on the form of humans, animals, and inanimate objects in order to deceive others. Merlina has certainly learned to mimic some strange sounds in order to get what she wants: one of her morning rituals is to make crow calls in order to get them to come down from the rooftops and the trees and play with her. She also has a knack for mimicking seagulls, but as far as I can tell, that's just to annoy them.

If you study diagrams and scans of bird anatomy you'll see how they make their incredible noises. They have these complex inner ears, and this voice box called the syrinx, which is like lips deep in their throats, worked by a set of muscles that shape the sound generated by a vibrating membrane called a tympanum. (Remember, ravens are oscines—songbirds. Oscines, humans, whales, dolphins, and some bats can demonstrate vocal learning.) But *why* they make these noises is another matter entirely.

It's important to remember that bird communication is not just about vocalization. Like us, they use a combination of voice and gestures and posture in order to make their point. Think about all the little signals that we're sending out when we're communicating, even when we think we're not. You have to learn to read the body language of a bird, just like you do with a human, if you want to understand the noises it makes. A raven uses its beak, for example, almost like a finger, to point out a food source to its mate or to other ravens nearby. It's a bit like learning the basic hand-signaling systems that we use in the army: deploy, halt, proceed. Observing and interpreting these various signs and signals from the ravens I can identify anger, hunger, fear, various warning calls, stress, anxiety, and depression. A raven's call indicates all sorts of basic needs—feed me, stay away, come here, help me. At school I remember we studied a lot of poems about birds and birdsong—Shelley on the skylark, Keats and Coleridge on the nightingale, Wordsworth, Thomas Hardy—but to be honest I think in all those poems the meaning of the birdsong was in the ear of the beholder. I certainly don't remember ever having studied a poem about raven song, let alone raven body language.

And I was definitely never taught that birds might be reading us as closely as we're reading them. The author Barry Lopez wrote a wonderful and strange book about ravens, *Desert Notes: Reflections in the Eye of a Raven*, in which he suggests the following: "If you want to know more about the raven: bury yourself in the desert so that you have a commanding view of the high basalt cliffs where he lives. Let only your eyes protrude. Do not blink—the movement will alert the raven to your continued presence." Always remember: ravens are watching you as closely as you're watching them.

Sometimes I can be over on the other side of the parade ground, for example, and Merlina will spot me and start calling to me. I don't even have to be in uniform for her to spot me. I can be walking past the ticket office on Tower Hill, which is *outside* of the Tower, and she'll recognize me and start calling. We have this "*k-nck k-nck*" call that we make to each other. She'll call for me, "*k-nck k-nck*." And I'll call back, "*k-nck k-nck*." She seems to find it reassuring. It's like us saying, "Hey, I'm over here if you need me." It can sometimes be a little embarrassing if I'm walking down Tower Hill and a human spots me, not in my uniform and making knocking sounds. I've had some strange looks.

Our full greeting ritual goes like this. First, Merlina shows her ears on the top of her head. (I know what you're thinking: where are a bird's ears? You have to look very closely. They're just to the side of the eyes.) Then there's that slight fluffing up of her head feathers, which gives her the unmistakable look of someone sporting a bad blow-dry. Then she bows her head and with some soft murmurings she spreads out her shoulders until her wings cross over at the back. Then I bow in return, mimicking her movements as closely as I can, though without the fluffing of the head feathers. And then the "*k-nck, k-nck*" sound, which I mimic, and then we take it in turns to display our friendship, ending only when we get bored with doing it.

I'm only communicating with Merlina like this because she was "humanized" before she came here. I certainly don't enjoy this kind of relationship with the other ravens. With Merlina, it's strictly a one-off and I can understand why people find it fascinating. When I post a video of us together, people are always amazed. And I'm glad. It's good for the ravens. I want the world to know more about them. But, as I've said, I don't believe in trying to make the ravens behave like pets.

I'm not interested in training them to do specific things. With the exception of Merlina, I might only touch the birds a dozen times a year when administering medicine, weighing them, or trimming the wings. And I have always, always refused to teach them to talk Human.

Accounts of talking ravens go back at least to the Emperor Augustus, who was apparently greeted in Rome after defeating Mark Antony by a man with a raven who proclaimed, "Hail Caesar, the victorious commander." (The man, it should be said, who was obviously a canny fellow, had also trained another bird to say "Hail Antony, the victorious commander." He was hedging his bets.) Dickens features a talking raven in his novel *Barnaby Rudge* (1841), who is based on his own pet raven, Grip, more of whom later. "Halloa, halloa, halloa!" squawks Grip. "What's the matter here! Keep up your spirits. Never say die. Bow wow wow. I'm a devil, I'm a devil, I'm a devil. Hurrah!" And in Hans Christian Andersen's famous story "The Snow Queen," a raven helps little Gerda search for her playmate Kai. "Listen," says the raven, "it is difficult to speak your language," and he asks Gerda if perhaps she can speak Ravenish instead. "No," replies Gerda, "I have not learned it, but my grandmother understands it, and she can speak gibberish too." I'll tell you what: Hans Christian Andersen was no fool.

Raven Thor was one of the last Tower ravens who'd been taught to croak out some phrases in English. Famously, as recorded in the Tower records on June 26, 2003, and widely reported elsewhere, during a visit to the Tower of London by

President Vladimir Putin of Russia, Thor amused Mr. Putin by wishing him a cheery "Good morning" as he walked up the stairs leading into the White Tower. It certainly is amusing, but that doesn't make it right. It's like when I was a kid and you'd go to the circus and you'd see the chimps pretending to have a tea party or the dogs dressed up and pushing prams or whatever. Birds are not toys: they're not objects for us to manipulate in whatever way we see fit. And having worked with talking ravens before—ones who squawk like parrots—I can tell you that there's nothing more embarrassing than walking around the Tower with a group of schoolchildren and suddenly having a raven hopping up to you and saying, "Bugger off! Bugger off!" Yeoman Warders haven't always taught the birds the most useful or appropriate of phrases. The obvious temptation to teach a raven "Nevermore," the immortal line from Edgar Allan Poe's poem "The Raven," is to be strongly resisted.

18

BIRD BRAINS

I don't teach the birds to speak Human or to squawk because—well, frankly, because they deserve better than that. Ravens are smart. Really, really smart. They have enormous brains for their small size. So big, in fact, that Nathan J. Emery, a primatologist turned ornithologist and the author of what is considered to be one of the best books in the world on bird behavior, *Bird Brain*—and therefore a person of not inconsiderable intelligence himself, and someone you would certainly expect to know—calls them "feathered apes." They're *that* smart. In relation to their body size, ravens have about the biggest brain of any birds in the world, rivaled only by parrots. (The brain sizes of different birds were measured by a Swiss zoologist by the name of Adolf Portmann in the 1940s. What a research project!)

In addition, the size of the raven's brain is matched by an amazing density of neurons. As Emery explains, it's a bird's brain anatomy that allows it to solve problems that it may have never previously encountered. According to Emery, birds possess four sorts of mental attributes: flexibility, imagination, prospection (thinking ahead), and causal reasoning. In particular I like the idea that imagination, which was once considered a uniquely human trait, allows birds to anticipate the outcome of their actions. If you go all the way back to the first century A.D., to Pliny the Elder, who was the first great naturalist, and also a soldier, a commander, and the author of *Naturalis Historia* (*Of Natural History*), he illustrates this aspect of avian intelligence with a story about a bird, thought to be a raven or a crow, who figured out that he could drop stones in a water bucket to raise the water level in order to get a sip of water. It's the same story that Aesop tells in "The Crow and the Pitcher." Pliny and Aesop could have been describing the Tower ravens. I see this sort of thing happening all the time, *every day*.

I've mentioned Munin's considerable skills and achievements at Raven KerPlunk, but that's just the beginning. The wily and intelligent Merlina rolls on her back and plays dead in order to get attention. She likes to play hide-and-seek with me. And as I mentioned, she is particularly adept at stealing food and other items from unsuspecting visitors. The other day she somehow managed to open a packet of twenty cigarettes, pulled them all out, and promptly destroyed them. Who needs Nicorette when you have Merlina! She snatches purses from young children and hides their coins. She once stole a child's small teddy bear and pulled off its head. That didn't go over so well. Like all of the other birds, she caches food, often digging up a piece of turf to bury what she doesn't need so that she can come back for it later. I've often observed the ravens watching a fellow bird bury a cache, and then sneaking along later to steal it, placing the turf back carefully to cover their tracks. I've also seen them lure many a poor pigeon into a deadly trap.

The pigeon strike is a classic display of raven guile and intelligence. If you've never seen it, it's really quite something to behold. It works like this. The ravens allow the pigeon to wander innocently on the grass bank by the White Tower, lulling it into a false sense of security. They then execute a simple pincer movement, of exactly the kind we learned as young infantrymen: one raven goes up on the bank and herds the pigeon down toward the other, who is hidden in a gully. And then they attack. Two ravens can kill and strip down a pigeon in a matter of minutes. Not long ago I was taking a tour around when I heard a lot of screaming and crying from people in the queues by the Jewel House. I rushed over and saw Erin and Rocky devouring a bird: they were actually eating the pigeon from the inside out while it was still alive. An incredible sight, though maybe not for everyone.

Observing the ravens over many years, I suppose I've become accustomed to their feeding methods. Their bills are like Swiss Army knives: they can use them to pick things up, rip things open, carry, probe. If you look carefully you'll see that the upper bill is ever so slightly hooked at the end, making it an even more effective weapon. You hear of ravens in the wild eating rodents and ducklings, and I know that in the

United States they're particularly partial to baby desert tortoises. I can only comment on what I've seen. When they're eating a mouse, for example, they'll usually remove the head first, the head being the most nutritious part, of course, and you never know how much time you're going to have with a meal in the wild, or in the wilds of Tower Green. It's just like being in the army, really.

Experts in avian cognition have designed all sorts of tests and experiments to measure birds' cognitive abilities and behavior, and I'm proud to say that our ravens at the Tower have assisted in many a scientific study. The consensus among the experts seems to be that ravens can carry out all sorts of tasks that it was previously thought only primates could handle. They exhibit tool use, for example, employing twigs or leaves held in their beaks to get at what they want. They have their own language. And they have a specific pecking order. Many renowned and respected scholars from all around the world have published and shared their reports of ravens showing off their extraordinary intelligence in the lab and in the wild. These various feats include snow bathing, assorted aerial acrobatics including flying upside down and doing barrel rolls, using objects to displace gulls from their nests, using rocks in nest defense, carrying food with their feet rather than with their bills, carrying their nestlings, catching doves in midair, and, incredibly, attacking reindeer!

The naturalist and keen observer of animal behavior Bernd Heinrich has spent his life studying ravens. In his book *Mind of the Raven* he writes, "Having now lived on intimate terms with ravens for many years, I have . . . seen amazing behavior that I had not read about in the more than fourteen hundred research reports and articles on ravens in the scientific literature, and that I could never have dreamed were possible. . . . Ultimately, knowing all that goes on in their brains is, like infinity, an unreachable destination." And the bestselling author David Quammen claims that what he calls the corvid "clan" is "so full of prodigious and quirky behavior that it cries out for interpretation not by an ornithologist but a psychiatrist."

I am not a zoologist, ornithologist, or psychiatrist, thank goodness, but as an amateur who's spent much of my adult life with ravens, I couldn't agree more: ravens are *phenomenally* intelligent and we will never know all of what goes on inside their heads. "Tha gliocas an ceann an fhitich," goes the old Scots Gaelic proverb—there is wisdom in a raven's head. I'm sure there is. I often try to see the Tower through the ravens' eyes: the sheer looming mass of the buildings, like cliffs, and the continual hubbub of sound, like the howl of the tundra; all that massive potential of playmates and the ever-present threat of predators. I try to imagine all the neurons firing in their brilliant little brains. I don't know but I'm guessing they stay put here, like me, partly because they get such a buzz out of the place.

•

I also often wonder about their emotions. They certainly seem to have the capacity to remember. When the former

Ravenmaster Derrick Coyle visited the Tower some seven years after leaving, for example, Merlina came straight over to him. It was as if he'd never been away. Seven years! There's doubtless some obvious explanation for this extraordinary behavior—something that Derrick did that attracted Merlina to him. But it also makes me wonder if she felt his absence, and what that feeling might be like for a bird. During my time as Ravenmaster I have seen ravens express joy and sorrow, pain and pleasure. I have seen them learn and remember and solve challenges involving principles of cause and effect. I know them to be capable of self-sacrifice, of caring, chivalry, and great courage. So do they possess complex cognitive abilities? Clearly. What is the exact extent of these abilities? I'm still finding out.

19

RAVENOLOGY

I see a large part of my role here as educating the public, which is perhaps ironic, given my own lack of formal schooling. This is not to say that I didn't go to good schools—to all my teachers in Dover, fair play to you for making an effort— but, as I mentioned, by the age of about fourteen I was barely attending. As a boy soldier in my teens, I still had to go to school two afternoons a week, though most of our lessons were what was called Military Studies, where we learned about the Cold War and the history of Russia's 3rd Shock Army, which might at any time attack the West. That was the only time in my life when I didn't bunk off school.

And yet now somehow I'm here, in a castle in the middle of London, and every spare moment I get, if I'm on a break, or early in the morning or late at night, I like to pore over histories and guides to the Tower and books about ravens. I've become a bit of a bookworm. I like nothing better than to be able to retreat to my little library in the Casemates in order to work through some raven-related three-pipe problem or concern. Why is Munin being aggressive? Why is Harris spending time on Tower Green? What new noise is Merlina mimicking?

The Yeoman Warders' houses in the Casemates are a bit like little dens or warrens—the word *casemates* literally refers to a fortified gun emplacement, consisting of rooms set deep within a defensive wall which are usually used as storerooms or strong rooms, and from which weapons are fired. No cannon is fired from here now, of course, nor are our homes used for the storage of weapons. These days, that would present some serious health and safety concerns for the Tower! No, an old gun emplacement may be an appropriate home for an old gunner, but I'm happy to say that our house, tucked into the northwest corner of the outer defensive wall, is a tranquil oasis of calm in the heart of London's metropolis. And in one little corner of this cozy corner is my office and library, what I think of as Raven HQ: my little nest.

I'm very lucky because a lot of people send me pictures and photographs and paintings of ravens. (I also get sent all sorts of raven lucky charms, badges, cups, wood carvings, raven-inspired clothes and calendars, *Game of Thrones* three-eyed raven toys, and some very nice raven-style decorated cakes and confectionery.) I keep all the paintings and pictures—every single one, right here. I could open a raven art gallery. Perhaps one day I will. I've got everything from children's drawings to big oil paintings and collages and sculptures—even one or two portraits of me with the ravens. The artist and sculptor Tim Shaw has spent quite a bit of time

here over the last couple of years with the ravens and produced some amazing work inspired by them. They're that
sort of bird. They just demand your attention.

One of the classic images of ravens in art is by Pieter
Bruegel the Elder, in his painting *The Triumph of Death*.
A raven sits perched on Death's horse as it pulls a cart along,
crushing the bodies of the dying under its wheels. It's not a
very cheery image. Shortly before he died, the famous French
illustrator, printmaker, and engraver Gustave Doré, best
known for his illustrations of the work of Dante and Milton,
produced a series of engravings for a special edition of Edgar
Allan Poe's poem "The Raven." They're also rather dis-
turbing. And when Lou Reed produced an album reimagin-
ing Poe's poem, he worked with the Italian artist Lorenzo
Mattotti on an accompanying graphic novel: also distinctly
weird. I've tried to do my own bit over the years to redress the
balance, spending a lot of my time photographing the ravens
and sharing them online, to show the birds in all their com-
plexity and beauty.

But of all the images of ravens that I've ever come across,
if you'd like to see some really astonishing raven art, I'd
suggest looking at the work of the Japanese photographer
Masahisa Fukase. His book *The Solitude of Ravens* consists
simply of black-and-white photographs of ravens. Fukase uses
his incredible skills as a photographer to produce images that
are often so blurry and murky and smudged that they could
almost be charcoal sketches. I think they come very close to
capturing the true majesty and mystery of the birds.

(And yes, in case you're wondering, I do have raven tattoos.

And no, I'm not going to show them to you. I'm rather fascinated by tattoo artists: the skill, the imagination, the attention to detail. Suffice it to say that one of my tattoos depicts
the raven as trickster, surrounded by the skulls of those
executed on Tower Green, and the other is of a raven in a
bowler hat, smoking a pipe, the raven as English gentleman.
If you're going to go to the trouble of getting a tattoo, you may
as well go the whole hog. I'm not one for the subtle tattoo—
what's the point?)

So when I'm not with the ravens, I'm in here reading
about them. As Ravenmaster I have long been collecting legends and stories about ravens from around the world. I have
books, files and files of raven-related newspaper cuttings, pho-
tocopies of articles, notes from Ravenmasters past, letters
from ornithologists, animal behavior scientists, and raven
researchers from around the world—in my amateur ornithological endeavors you might say that I have been ornithiv-
orous, studying ornithomancy, ornithophily, and all things
ornithic. There are stories and legends about ravens from
North America, South America, Asia, Europe, Africa. The
raven features in the myths and legends of the Romans, the
Greeks, the Celts, the ancient Egyptians, the Native Americans, and the Scandinavians. There are more learned books
and articles on what I call Ravenology than anyone could possibly read in a lifetime. But as far as I can tell, the one thing
that unites all these stories is the paradoxical nature of the
raven—paradoxical in a sense that, say, puffins or nightingales
simply are not. (And the Tower ravens are more paradoxical

than most: birds who live in a palace, waited on by human servants. I mean, come on!) Ravens are associated with evil as much as they are with good. They are harbingers of doom, yet they are creators and protectors. They are double-hatted in their very nature. Perhaps this is why so many cultures throughout history have been fascinated by the figure of the raven: in their capacity for good and ill, they remind us of ourselves.

The stories and legends of the raven are so beautiful and so strange. I think of them often when I'm out observing Merlina and the others. Very often ravens are figured as agents or messengers of God, or of the gods. In the Bible, there are ravens who bring the prophet Elijah bread and meat. In Tibet, ravens and crows are regarded as messengers of the Supreme Being. In the mythology of the Haida Indians of the Pacific Northwest Coast, Raven created the world and made humans out of rocks and leaves. In other Pacific Northwest cultures—among the Tlingit—it is believed that wearing the headgear of ravens and crows enables the wearer to journey to the land of the dead and return with a person's soul. Noah sent out a raven to scout for land, just as in the Epic of Gilgamesh (in a brilliant story in which Utnapishtim and his wife survive a flood and send out a dove, which returns, and then a swallow, which does likewise, and then finally a raven, which never returns, and so Utnapishtim knows that he and his family will be saved). According to the Saga of Flóki, the Vikings discovered Iceland after Flóki released three ravens from his ship: the first never returned, the second came back to the ship, and the third flew west and Flóki followed. Odin, the Norse deity, had a pair of ravens, one named Hugin (from the Old Norse, meaning "thought") and the other Munin (from the Old Norse, meaning "memory"—fitting for our Munin, who never forgets that she doesn't like me), and every day he sent out his two ravens to see what was happening in the world and then they'd report back. They were like his secret police.

Great stories all.

But the raven legend closest to my heart is obviously the story of the ravens of the Tower. This is a story that's been told and written about many times—though never, I think, by a serving Ravenmaster. It is as strange and perplexing in its way as any of the great legends of the raven from around the world.

What follows is my take on the legend of the ravens at the Tower.

20

THE LEGEND OF THE RAVENS AT THE TOWER

The story goes that Charles II was once visiting the Tower of London after the restoration of the monarchy to survey a new building. At the time, a young astronomer named John Flamsteed was using a room in the round turret house at the top of the White Tower for his observations of the stars and the moon, but he had found that the nesting ravens rather obstructed his view and interfered with his work. Flamsteed asked Charles II if he might be able to get rid of "those confounded ravens." Charles, being a decent sort of a king, readily agreed, until someone pointed out that the birds had always been at the Tower and were an important symbol of the city and the monarchy, and that getting rid of them would therefore seem like rather a bad omen. Mindful no doubt that both the city and the monarchy had had a bit of a run of bad luck recently, what with his father Charles I having been executed, and there having been a terrible plague in London in 1665, and then the Great Fire of London in 1666, Charles promptly issued a royal decree, commanding that instead of banishing the birds, at least six ravens should be kept at the Tower forevermore. If the ravens should ever leave, the kingdom would fall.

I tell this wonderful story to visitors. The other Yeoman Warders tell this wonderful story to visitors. The story is repeated in books and articles. It's a good story. It's a great story. It's an important story. It is a part of our national heritage. But in all my research over the years in Raven HQ, assisted by the incredible resources of the Tower's library and my archives, in all the years I've been looking and searching, and with all the experts I've consulted, I have been able to find no mention whatsoever of the legend of the ravens at the Tower before the late nineteenth century. Let me just say that again: no mention of the legend of the ravens at the Tower until the late nineteenth century. Nothing, nada, zilch. Not a croak. Nothing about Charles II and his decree. Nothing about Flamsteed and the confounded ravens. Nothing about the kingdom falling if the ravens should ever leave the Tower.

The truth is that there was no Royal Decree protecting the ravens issued by Charles II, though there was admittedly a Royal Warrant issued in June 1675, which provided John Flamsteed, who became the first Royal Astronomer, with the funding to set up a proper observatory in Greenwich. The Royal Observatory was established for the purpose of "rectifieing the Tables of the motions of the Heavens, and the places of the fixed stars, so as to find out the so much desired

Longitude of places for Perfecteing the Art of Navigation"—
so it's possible that the confounded ravens played a small
part in the history of astronomy and navigation in this country, simply by being so bloody annoying that Flamsteed had
to move out to Greenwich to get away from them!

Not only is there no evidence of ravens having played an
important part in the history of the Tower before the late
nineteenth century, there is barely any mention of the ravens
at the Tower in the historical record before then *at all*. Take the
old *Authorized Guide to the Tower of London* by W. J. Loftie,
published in its second edition in 1888. Any mention of the
ravens? No. Nothing. The ever popular and magisterial *Her
Majesty's Tower*, by William Hepworth Dixon, first published
in 1869? Nothing. Even William Benham's *The Tower of
London*, published in 1906, mentions not the mighty raven.
One of the first official Tower guidebooks to mention the
birds is Colonel E. H. Carkeet-James's *His Majesty's Tower of
London*, which wasn't published until 1950, and even then the
birds are seen largely as an annoyance. "They are not popular
with the residents of the Tower," according to the Colonel.
"They tear up the grass, flowers create an urge to destroy,
they pick out the putty from windows and the lead from the
diamond leaded lights in the Chapel Royal of St. Peter ad
Vincula. Few motor cars are safe from their marauding and
they find a strange fascination in ladies' silk stockings."

As far as I've been able to ascertain, from my own research and from the work of various historians and scholars,
the first significant depiction of the ravens at the Tower wasn't

until 1883, in an article in the *Pictorial World* newspaper on July 14, which has a drawing of what certainly looks like a raven by the entrance to the Chapel of St. Peter ad Vincula, near the plaque commemorating the executions on Tower Green. In the same year there was also a children's book, *London Town*, by Felix Leigh, illustrated by Thomas Crane and Ellen Houghton, which tells the story, in verse, of a young girl named Prue touring London with her parents. The book includes a drawing of Prue and her parents at the Tower, observing a little girl outside Beauchamp Tower, looking rather frightened at the sight of two ravens and clinging to a Yeoman Warder. The text accompanying the drawing seems to be the first significant mention of the ravens at the Tower.

Among the sights of London Town
Which little visitors wish to view,
The Tower stands first, and its great renown
Has, you will notice, attracted Prue.

At a well-known spot, to Miss Prue's surprise,
Some fine old ravens are strutting about.
If upon the picture a glance you cast,
You will know the ravens next time, no doubt.

The red-coated guard who's watching here
Is called a Beefeater—fancy that!
And Prue discovers, as she draws near,
A child by his side who is round and fat.

"Father and Mother, pray come here,"
In tones so pleasant, laughs lively Prue:
"You've shown *me* things that are odd and queer,
A Beefeater's baby I'll show *you!*"

After Prue and her parents, the accounts of the ravens at the Tower start to proliferate. There is raven contagion! In *Birds in London*, published in 1898, W. H. Hudson claims, "For many years past two or three ravens have usually been kept at the Tower of London." And so the stories begin to grow.

You can see the beginnings of the legend of the ravens growing and blossoming before your very eyes in the work of Major-General Sir George Younghusband, of the Guides Cavalry, a formidable soldier who served in the Second Afghan War, the Mahdist War, the Third Burmese War, the Second Boer War, and the First World War, and who was appointed Keeper of the Jewel House at the Tower in 1917. In his book *The Tower from Within*, Younghusband provides a comprehensive guide to life at the Tower, its history and traditions as understood at the beginning of the twentieth century. According to Younghusband:

Round and about the site of the ancient scaffold, or sitting silent on a bench near by, may be seen the historic ravens of the Tower. No doubt when forests grew close up to the moat the turrets of the old Tower made an ideal place in which ravens could build their

nests, and rear future generations of Tower ravens.
But as the city grew around and the forests receded,
and with them fields for forage, the ravens would no
longer nest or breed in their old haunts. They have
therefore since then from time to time had to be replaced by new blood from outside. The present birds
were given to the Tower by Lord Dunraven, and one
of them is now of considerable age.

It would be of historic interest if those whose ancestors have suffered at the Tower would send from
their homes successors to the old ravens, as they die
off, and thus maintain a very old tradition in a man-
ner well in keeping.

It seems likely that the "very old tradition" that Younghusband mentions was no more than thirty or forty years
old at the time. Nonetheless, a few years later, in 1924, when
he published another book about the Tower, *A Short History
of the Tower of London*, he elaborated upon the theme of the
Tower's ancient raven traditions:

Walking about on the Tower Green, or perhaps
perched on the steps of the White Tower, may be seen
a few ravens, three or four, sometimes five. These are
the Ravens of the Tower and as much part of it as
are the Yeomen Warders. What their origin may
have been is lost in the mists of antiquity, but possibly
when the Tower stood alone—a rock-like edifice

The true guardians of the Tower of London.

Visit of HM Queen Elizabeth II, Dedication of the Chapel Royal of
St. Peter ad Vincula, October 16, 2014.

OPPOSITE: Yeoman Warder Christopher Skaife, of Her Majesty's Royal
Palace and Fortress the Tower of London, and member of the Sovereign
Body Guard of the Yeoman Guard Extraordinary.

Aerial view of the Tower of London.

Blood Swept Lands and Seas of Red.

Biscuits and blood.
Bon appétit!

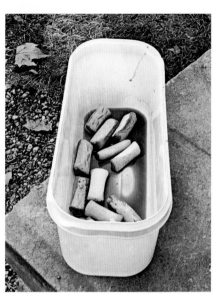

Raven: Handle
with Care.

Up close and personal.

Feeding the pigeons in Trafalgar Square.

I may be a raven, but I'm a lion amongst birds.

The Raven Memorial.

amidst the fields and forests which then surrounded
it—ravens built their nests in its high turrets. An historian mentions that they were gazing on the scene
when Queen Anne Boleyn was executed. Perhaps
after the ravens ceased to nest in such unquiet
surroundings as the Tower they formed part of the
menagerie maintained by Kings of England in the
Tower as one of their regal fancies. Whatever their
origin may have been, they are now maintained on
the strength of the garrison, are duly enlisted—
having an attestation card as has a soldier—and
daily receive their ration of raw meat and other deli-
cacies issued by the Yeoman Warder in whose charge
they are placed. [. . .] A whole chapter could be filled
with stories about the Tower Ravens and their adventures and escapades and amusements, and these
can be gathered from any of the kindly Yeoman
Warders whom the visitor may meet, but here un-
happily there is no more space for them.

We have a saying in the military, "Pull up a sandbag and
I'll tell you a story," and I suggest at this point you do exactly
that: pull up a sandbag and this kindly Yeoman Warder will
offer you his own take on the history of the ravens at the
Tower.

Personally, I have no doubt that ravens have long been
present here. The White Tower was for many centuries one
of the tallest buildings in London, and what with Smithfield

Market nearby, and the amount of rubbish and decaying flesh that would anyway have been bobbing its way downstream in the River Thames, the Tower would have been an ideal spot for ravens to congregate and nest. In a letter written by Sir Walter Raleigh to Robert Cecil, 1st Viscount Cranborne, in the winter of 1604–1605, while he was imprisoned in the Bloody Tower, Raleigh implores his friend to "save this quarter which remaineth from the ravens of this time which feed on all things." Poor Sir Walter was clearly having a bad day when he wrote the letter, though the good news is that he survived his imprisonment in the Tower and was in fact pardoned by the King in 1617 and granted permission to go off in search of El Dorado—though admittedly he was then beheaded in the Old Palace Yard at the Palace of Westminster in 1618! Anyway, his plea to Robert Cecil to save his wasted body from the ravens suggests that there were indeed ravens in and around the Tower at the time.

What we know for sure is that the ravens only became a *notable* and *remarkable* feature at the Tower sometime in the late 1800s. Perhaps it was simply because the raven population throughout the rest of the country had declined so sharply, having been hunted down and killed as vermin, that the few remaining birds at the Tower became worthy of comment. But I think there's more to it. Here's what I think happened. This is the unproven and untested Skaife Theory about the creation of the legend of the ravens at the Tower, derived from many years of research and experience working at the Tower: you could also call it the Yeoman Warder Theory. The Yeoman Warder Theory is based on an understanding not only of the nature and behavior of the ravens, but also on the nature and behavior of human beings. The Yeoman Warder Theory is that it was the Yeoman Warders *themselves* who had a hand in inventing the legend of the ravens at the Tower, and for their own profit.

Imagine the scene.

It's the 1880s. The Tower has begun opening its gates to ever greater numbers of the general public, to the great unwashed, accepting paying visitors to the most notorious prison and fortress in the land, with its gruesome history of murder, executions, and torture. And here you are among them—washed, unwashed, whatever—waiting in anticipation for the Tower's ancient wooden gates to open and your Beefeater guide to meet you. Slowly the gates begin to part, creaking and groaning from almost a thousand years of use. From behind the great gate appears an old man leaning on a twisted wooden cane, wearing a dirty dark blue uniform decorated with scarlet and braid, an odd medal or two pinned to his chest. On his head is a curious hat, set at a jaunty angle. There's a strong whiff of gin and stale tobacco about him.

"Give me a shilling and you can come in," he growls. "And I will tell you our dark, dark secrets." You hand over your coin, he shoves it in his pocket, and then he turns and hobbles back inside the Tower. "Follow me!" he cries. "And keep up!"

So you enter through the gates and follow him as he begins to recount his dreadful tales of the Tower's history.

As you reach the Traitor's Gate, he stops and turns. "Do you dare to go farther inside?"

You nod, fearful and excited, and he rubs his fingers together. "In which case . . . I will need another coin or two." He scowls.

And so it goes—the deeper you penetrate inside the Tower, the deeper his pockets are filled with your hard-earned cash. Until at last, at the scaffold site on Tower Green, the ancient Yeoman Warder claims actually to have seen the ghost of Anne Boleyn! And to have heard the pitiful whimpers of the two boy princes, murdered deep within the Bloody Tower! And to himself have felt the shudders as the murdered Queens of England laid down their heads and the sharp edge of cold metal fell upon their dainty necks! And there—he points, finally, triumphantly—are the ravens, reminders of our dark past, souls of the departed, the very souls of those who were executed on the private scaffold site on Tower Green! "Witness the ravens! Here since the beginning of time! Here since Anne Boleyn herself was executed!"

What a way to enhance the story! Living, breathing representations of the life of the Tower. And all it would have taken would have been to trim the feathers of a few ravens and feed them the occasional scraps, and that'll be another penny, sir!

Enough of my cockamamie theories. Back to the present. There's cleaning to be done. Wherever there are humans or animals, there is *always* cleaning to be done.

21

BLOOD SWEPT LANDS
AND SEAS OF RED

If you go on any army base anywhere in the world on the eve of an inspection, you'll find soldiers frantically cleaning, fixing, and painting things. We used to have to paint everything in our regimental colors—yellow and royal blue. Horrible. Rocks, tree trunks, everything. Basically, if it moved, and indeed if it didn't move, we cleaned it or we painted it, or both. You always want yours to be a good tidy unit—shiny boots, freshly pressed uniforms, all your kit in good order— but more important, it's this sort of discipline that'll save you on the battlefield. Making sure that everything works and is clean and ready, and that you know how it works and how to work it, having practiced it again and again until you can practice it no more, and then practicing it again and again until you *really* can't practice it anymore, and so on, eventually forms habits that become instincts. The basic disciplines of cleaning and tidying and good old-fashioned spit and polish also instill in you the art of being intensely observant. A good soldier will always notice when something's changed, when something's out of place, and when something's wrong. And these are skills that might one day save your life.

So it's not surprising that one of the first things I learned with Ravenmaster Derrick Coyle was the importance of cleaning the cages. Derrick was old-school: when it came to raven care, everything had to be perfect. I do my absolute best to maintain the same standards. These days I undertake a deep clean of the enclosures about once a month, disinfecting everything, hosing and raking over the gravel, making sure every single piece of cached food is cleared, checking for any damage to the wire or the wood, oiling all the moving parts, checking the perches and the night boxes. And every day I go through a simple clean and tidy routine. Is everything in place? Is everything where it should be? Everything in order? The same routine, 365 days a year. In fact, I would say that a large part of being the Ravenmaster is being persistent, punctual, and a bit of a perfectionist.

But for all the necessary routine and monotony there are of course some days at the Tower that stand out—the special occasions, events, and ceremonies that are unusual and that you never forget.

For me, one of those days and one of those occasions was August 16, 2014.

You probably know the story of the ceramic poppies at the Tower. To commemorate the centenary of the beginning of the First World War, Historic Royal Palaces commissioned the artists Paul Cummins and Tom Piper to create a piece of art. They came up with the idea of making a spectacular sea of ceramic red poppies, precisely 888,246, the number of British and Commonwealth soldiers who were killed during the war. With the help of thousands of volunteers from all over the world, including my daughter, during a period of 117 days between the seventeenth of July—the first full day of Britain's involvement in the war—and the eleventh of November, the Tower's moat was filled with poppies, each one representing a soldier killed in action. It was the largest-ever installation work in the U.K., titled *Blood Swept Lands and Seas of Red*. If you've never seen it, you need to look it up. It is simply astonishing. The task of arranging the poppies was in itself immense and required a vast amount of coordination from the project team, managed by John Brown, the then Deputy Governor to the Tower, and Yeoman Warder Jim Duncan RVM, now my Yeoman Sergeant, and the efforts of all the Historic Royal Palaces staff and Tower residents. Truly a military operation.

This remarkable work of art became an important site for visitors to congregate and to pay their respects. People came to leave flowers and photos tied to the railings. They came day and night, day in, day out. I remember my wife and I would sometimes wake in the morning to the incredible sound of the cheers from the awaiting crowds when the floodlights were turned on to illuminate the poppies. I've never heard anything like it. And through the narrow slits of our house in the Casemates you could see the vivid red of the poppies shining, bathing the Tower in this beautiful, terrible glow. It was surreal. For those of us living at the Tower, *Blood Swept Lands and Seas of Red* dominated our lives. There were occasions when we couldn't leave the Tower because of the sheer volume of people gathered outside.

As part of the commemorations, the public was asked to nominate family members who had been killed in action during the war, and every evening at the Tower, at sunset, a Yeoman Warder would walk out into the sea of poppies and read out 180 names, followed by the traditional call of the Last Post.

On Saturday, August 16, 2014, it was my turn to read the names.

I rehearsed all day. I was determined to pronounce each name correctly. I didn't want to let down any of those fallen soldiers and their families.

•

When sunset came I dressed in my uniform, with my collection of medals proudly pinned to my chest, and made my way along the narrow path that meandered its way through the sea of ceramic poppies. The crowd was gathered in silence, as they were every night.

I put on my reading glasses, took the list of names so that I could see them clearly in the shadows, and looked up at the crowd. I took a deep breath and for a moment I remembered my own service career and all those who had gone before me.

I remembered driving back to the barracks from our final exercise during training. We were in an old army coach, all the weapons in the back—rifles, machine guns, antitank weapons. And a lorry drove into us at high speed. I was sitting toward the back of the coach. The lorry driver was badly injured. We tried to put a field dressing on his wounds, putting into practice our recently acquired first-aid skills. When we had our passing-out parade there were a lot of us in wheelchairs and on crutches. That's when I realized that we weren't playing soldiers anymore.

•

I remembered when we finished our training and finally joined our regiments. I became a part of the Queen's Division, which was made up of the Queen's Regiment, the Royal Anglian and the Royal Regiment of Fusiliers: a proud moment. I was in the 3rd Battalion of the Queen's Regiment, until we were amalgamated with the Royal Hampshire Regiment in 1992 and we all became the Princess of Wales's Royal Regiment, known as Di's Guys, after Diana, Princess of Wales. I met the princess a couple of times. She was our Colonel-in-Chief—a lovely lady. The day she died I had just been posted as a Drum Major instructor to the Infantry Training Centre at Catterick in North Yorkshire. I remember arriving and hearing the news and all of us just sitting in the mess, staring at the television in disbelief.

I remembered my very first posting with the regiment to Bad Fallingbostel in Germany, Lower Saxony. I was eighteen. Ours was a mechanized battalion, so we spent a lot of our time as infantry soldiers on exercises in army personnel carriers in and around Germany, and a lot of our time as drummers playing at beer festivals. I was young and enjoying my new life, making new friends, many of whom are still my best friends a full thirty-five years later. It was at the time of the Cold War, and Germany was our playground.

But then, almost as soon as we arrived at the battalion base in Germany, we started what was called the Northern Ireland package—a two-week training course where we learned riot training and street patrols, preparing us for deployment to Northern Ireland. And then we were deployed. Which was a bit of a shock.

The early 1980s were a terrible time in Northern Ireland. We flew into Aldergrove, and within forty-eight hours I was out on top cover in an armored Land Rover, getting petrol-bombed in Andersonstown. I remember thinking to myself, "What the hell am I doing here?" That first four-month tour in Belfast was a rude awakening. I was part of a four-man team patrolling the streets, all of us blokes from London and the southeast of England, with not a clue about what was happening in Northern Ireland, but trying to do our best, to do our duty, many of us just eighteen or nineteen years old, and we had about eleven contacts in that first tour as a battalion. It was hard. It was dangerous. We were pretty unpopular, out on patrols, driving around in the Pigs—the classic old armored personnel carriers—looking for IEDs, doing house searches, sangar duties, stagging on, "p checking" people. It sounds silly, but that was one of the hardest things, p checking—asking people for their papers. We were only teenagers, after all, and there we were asking people for their personal details, checking up on them. Understandably, not all of them responded warmly to our requests.

There were some close shaves. Snipers, bullets, bombs. I remember eating breakfast one morning in a police station and a grenade coming over the wall and the shrapnel hitting the table right in front of me. This was a long way from playing soldiers in my back garden as a lad. When I married I ended up living off base in Northern Ireland with my wife. She was twenty-one, I was twenty-two. We were just kids, really. Two young English kids way out of our comfort zone, and—I'll be honest—it was not a good time to be a British soldier living off base in Northern Ireland. We were subjected to some pretty nasty stuff—threats, intimidation, more bombs. That's how terrorism works, after all. We just tried to get on with it.

We had our good times as well. I remember I was in Turf Lodge once and this little girl came up to me and said "Hey, mister, my mum prays for you every night." Another time, just off the Falls Road these little old ladies invited us in for a cup of tea and a piece of cake. They couldn't have been more kind. It was those acts of kindness that made you think what you were doing was worthwhile, that made you realize the importance of every small gesture and remark.

Being in the military is a strange life, but I wouldn't have missed it for the world. In the army you work together, you live together, you grieve together, you celebrate together. The army was my family.

And so I looked at the list of names and began to read.

On the exact spot among the poppies where I was standing to read, one hundred years ago, one of the very first battalions of the volunteer army began to be raised from the City of London, from the streets round and about the Tower. In just a matter of days 1,600 young men had joined what became the 10th Battalion, Royal Fusiliers, known as the Stock Exchange Battalion. Many of them were killed on the Western Front.

As I read I thought of all the people who gave their lives so that we might enjoy the freedoms we have today. To read 180 names and their regiments takes some time. But to read the names and regiments of all 888,246 British and Commonwealth soldiers who were killed in the First World War would take weeks.

•

"They shall grow not old, as we that are left grow old: / Age shall not weary them, nor the years contemn. / At the going down of the sun and in the morning / We will remember them." I read aloud Laurence Binyon's poem of remembrance, and during the Last Post, I had to fight back the tears. "Stand down soldier, your duty is done." And I turned and made my way back through the poppies.

Without a doubt, it was the one of the proudest moments of my life, to take part in such a profound act of remembrance.

And I'm glad that I got to share it with Merlina.

One fine sunny morning, as the volunteers were working in shifts placing the poppies around the moat, Merlina decided to fly out of the Tower to find out what all the fuss was about.

"Chris, I think Merlina's been spotted outside of the Tower near the ticket office," came a message from the radio.

"Roger, last caller, I'll go and take a look," I replied.

We get a fair few reports of our ravens sighted outside the Tower, normally by members of Historic Royal Palaces staff on their way to work or leaving at the end of the day, and from concerned and conscientious members of the public, aware of the legend that the kingdom will fall should the ravens ever leave the Tower. Luckily most of the calls are false alarms: the ravens turn out to be crows.

But on this occasion the report was absolutely correct. Merlina had indeed left the Tower and had been spotted by a vigilant member of the public. If she ever leaves the safety of her territory on Tower Green—normally because she's being threatened by one of the more dominant ravens—I'll usually find her perched on a fence along the Tower Wharf, watching the boats going up and down the Thames. The Wharf was of course at one time used as the quayside to load stores and munitions in and out of the Tower, and as the riverside entrance for the highest-ranking dignitaries and visitors, and indeed for those poor souls being brought by river from trial at the Guildhall or the Palace of Westminster to Traitors' Gate, to imprisonment or execution. Nowadays it's just a very pleasant walkway along a cobbled path, and a great place to get a coffee and a photo of Tower Bridge.

Today, though, Merlina was not on the Wharf. She'd gone straight to see the poppies of *Blood Swept Lands and Seas of*

Red. I made my way toward the front entrance, past the Middle Tower and the long line of visitors showing their tickets and getting their bags checked before entry to the Tower grounds. I walked up the small incline of Tower Hill, a route that many an unfortunate prisoner would have been taken on their short journey from the Tower to the public execution site.

It's not hard to spot a wayward raven outside the Tower: they tend to attract a bit of a crowd, with cameras and phones furiously clicking and a great hubbub, everyone wondering how and why such an extraordinarily large black bird is sitting innocently on some bench or fence preening itself, or snacking on crisps from a bin. So I just followed the crowds and soon found Merlina. She'd positioned herself on an old iron fence overlooking the moat, cronking loudly at the volunteers who were busy placing the poppies down below.

To catch and capture a raven in full view of the public is a tricky business and to be avoided if at all possible, since it requires not only a cool head and steady nerves but quite a bit of luck. My first piece of advice to anyone finding themselves in such a predicament would be to stay cool and to pretend you have total control of the situation, which you most certainly do not. Like it or not, you're about to become a star on YouTube. If you are a small round middle-aged man dressed in a wide-brimmed bonnet, wearing a royal blue and scarlet dress—it's called a tabard, people, for goodness sake!—and you're going to attempt to catch a raven, I can pretty much guarantee that you're about to be photographed, videoed, and live-streamed on every social media platform imaginable. Prepare yourself: you're going to go viral.

My second piece of advice would be to make your way slowly—SLOWLY!—and casually toward the offending raven. Do not attempt to move or scatter the crowd—they make the perfect cover for your approach. As you steadily navigate your way through, remember to reassure everyone that you know what you're doing.

Merlina was clearly having a lovely day out and certainly did not want to be caught and returned to Tower Green. One more piece of advice: Don't think for one minute that you're just going to be able to walk up to your raven and sweep her off her talons by looking lovingly into her dark-brown beady eyes, and gather her up in your big strong arms and take her back home. This is not how raven rescue works. You need to be cunning. You need to be stealthy. You need to be quick. You need to pretend you're not interested, that you just happen to be in the vicinity and then, with the speed of a striking cobra, you need to grab her when she least expects it. And *that* is how to catch a miscreant raven, ladies and gentlemen!

I caught and held tight to Merlina and I could hear the people in the crowd murmuring, some in approval, some in disapproval, some expressing sheer disbelief. As I returned with Merlina to Tower Green, I didn't have it in me to scold her for escaping—in fact, I was glad she'd seen the poppies. Like us, she'd have had plenty of ancestors who spent their days on battlefields, so at a time of remembrance it seemed appropriate that she was there—all part of the circle of life.

22

MY MISTRESS' EYES
ARE RAVEN BLACK

Since I'm an old soldier, I suppose you'd expect me to be happier talking about war than love. And here at the Tower we certainly have plenty of war stories to tell, tales of death and derring-do, and tales of tragedy. The three soldiers from the Black Watch shot at dawn on Tower Green in 1743, accused of being ringleaders in a mutiny. The rioting mobs of peasants who laid siege to the Tower during the Peasants' Revolt in 1381. Fifteen direct hits on the Tower from high explosives during the Second World War, with twenty-three people killed.

But the history of the Tower is in fact as much about love as it is about war: Anne Boleyn and Catherine Howard accused of adultery and beheaded; the Princess, later Queen Elizabeth and the great love of her life Robert Dudley both imprisoned here at the same time; Katherine Grey incarcerated for her secret marriage to Edward Seymour.

I've never been much of a ladies' man myself. I had a few

girlfriends when I was still at school, but once I was in the army, it was different. I was really concentrating on my job and my career and had no intention of getting married. Until, that is, I met the woman who would become my wife—and it was love at first sight. Like anything else, sometimes love just comes along and hits you out of nowhere. It's the same for the ravens.

Ravens have long been known to be monogamous and to stick with a partner for life, though my observations would suggest that when one of a raven pair dies the surviving partner often takes up with another raven almost immediately. Most of the Tower ravens form strong bonds and attachments with one another. They pair up either as partners or as friends, male to male and female to female, for protection and companionship. Our raven pairs hang around together during the day, they sleep close together, and they continually chat to each other and preen one another. They might even attack other pairs, and they certainly hunt in pairs. Merlina—as always—being the exception.

For many years Merlina used to allow another female raven named Hugine to hang around with her. They weren't partners—they weren't preening each other in the way male and female ravens do—but Merlina seemed to enjoy or least tolerate Hugine's company, chatting with her and occasionally sharing food with her. Merlina seemed to be saying, "Look, I don't want you too close, but I don't mind if you happen to be around." Sadly, Hugine died suddenly in 2016, cause unknown, though it was likely something she'd picked up to eat that didn't agree with her. For the Ravenmaster, this proved a great challenge. Immediately after the death of Hugine, Merlina protected the body: she wouldn't let anyone go near it to pick it up and remove it. She paced around the area, constantly returning to peck at Hugine's face, as if trying to wake her. It was heartbreaking to watch. In the days and weeks that followed she would often leave her home territory around Tower Green, which is most unlike her, and would turn her back to the public and even to me if I approached. She began to slouch and drop her head down low, as if in mourning or despair. In the end, I had to intervene because she'd stopped eating. I put her in the new enclosure with the other ravens in an attempt to break her depressive cycle and to keep her occupied. It took a few weeks of me spending lots of time with her, but finally she recovered and went back to her usual activities on Tower Green. I'd read about ravens mourning, but to see it for myself was quite extraordinary.

•

Almost as extraordinary, in fact, as the time Munin fell in love with a monkey.

In 2010 the Tower installed more than a dozen animal sculptures by the artist Kendra Haste, to celebrate the history of the Royal Menagerie. The creatures are made of galvanized wire and represent the various animals that the Tower has been home to over the past six hundred years: there are lions, a full-size polar bear, an elephant's head, and a troop of baboons who sit up on the walls, guarding the exit of the Jewel House.

"Chris, have you seen up there?" asked the Jewel House Warden one day, pointing toward the roof of the Brick Tower. "I think one of your ravens has taken a fancy to one of our monkeys."

"Oh no," I sighed.

Munin's then partner had recently disappeared, and in her grief, Munin seemed to have fixated on the monkey. She stayed on the roof of the Brick Tower, sitting next to the inanimate monkey for a full three days and nights before finally flying down and playing hide-and-seek with former Ravenmaster Rocky Stones and me, his clueless assistant. For hours we hunted for Munin, high and low, in every dark recess of the Tower, before catching up with her merrily hopping across the floodlit moat. We immediately placed her under close arrest, mostly to protect her from the other ravens who might have sensed her weakness after the loss of her partner and attempted to exert dominance over her, but also, quite frankly, for being such a nuisance!

Of course, as soon as we released her, she simply went straight back to the damned monkey. For the next few months she would fly and climb up one of the service ladders every single day in order get alongside it and croak away in a deep and meaningful one-way conversation. She would also delicately tap the monkey with her beak, as if to say "Hey! I'm here. Come on, talk to me, I'm lonely." I often wondered what she must have thought when the monkey failed to answer. Again and again we would climb up the Tower and encourage her to find another partner among the other ravens, but it made no difference. Every day she would return to the monkey. It was an obsession.

Eventually she just grew tired of talking to the silent metal monkey and life returned to normal. But if you ever visit the Tower, take the time to make your way around to the North Wall and stop just before you enter the Brick Tower. Pause and look up and you'll see the metal monkey—and you might ponder for a moment the mysteries of love and loss.

23

BIRDS AND BOOKS

When I'm not busy wrangling actual ravens, I like to catch up on a bit of essential "raven admin" and meet with any journalists, photographers, artists, writers, and film crews interested in the birds. Sound glamorous? Think again. Ravens are a law unto themselves—and they're not here for our entertainment.

I recall filming a sequence one balmy evening on Tower Green for a documentary called *Natural Curiosities* with the great Sir David Attenborough. Sir David was doing a small piece on tool use among corvids. I remember he was sitting on a bench and the director asked if a raven could sit next to him during the sequence. As so often, I had to explain that the ravens at the Tower are in no way tame or indeed biddable, but we did our best. We tried to tempt a raven down. And we tried again. And again. And again. But alas, no raven would come into the shot and sit on the bench next to Sir David.

So several weeks later, the poor chap and the film crew

had to return to do it all over. This time we just about managed to get Sir David in a shot with one of the birds—and my great claim to fame is that I'm in the shot too. The director said I was by far the best silent Yeoman Warder extra they'd ever worked with.

"More has probably been written about the raven than about any other bird," according to the great Bernd Heinrich, in *Ravens in Winter*—and judging by the number of journalists and writers we have in, he may be right. I'm certainly conscious, as I chronicle my own experiences, that I am merely adding to a vast library of books about birds. There are books about hawks, there are books about snow geese, books about kestrels; you've got Gerard Manley Hopkins's windhover, you've got W. B. Yeats's wild swans at Coole, Wallace Stevens's blackbird, John Keats's "Ode to a Nightingale"—writers seem to be able to identify with cuckoos, owls, parrots, swans, albatrosses, you name it.

Birds clearly function as important symbols in our lives. I don't want to sound too much like a psychoanalyst here, but maybe in writing about our birds here at the Tower I'm subconsciously making the ravens into the image of me, and me into the image of them. It happens to all of us: we think we're describing the world when in fact we're describing ourselves.

What I really don't like, though, is the one-dimensional representation of ravens. The English writer Edmund Spenser—who was born and brought up near Tower Hill, as it happens—has a long, long, long poem, *The Faerie Queene*, in which ravens are described as "The hateful messengers of heavy things, / Of death and dolour telling sad tidings," which in my opinion just about sums up the whole of English literature's rather limited appreciation of the raven. (Could Spenser have seen ravens at the Tower? Professors of medieval and Renaissance literature, do let me know.) You get ravens aplenty in Shakespeare, of course, but again he tends to use them as omens of death, dying, and doom. In *Macbeth*, Lady Macbeth says, "The raven himself is hoarse / That croaks the fatal entrance of Duncan / Under my battlements." In *Julius Caesar*, when Cassius imagines his defeat he imagines "ravens, crows, and kites" that "Fly o'er our heads and downward look on us, / As we were sickly prey." Et cetera et cetera.

There are exceptions, thank goodness, to this one-dimensional take. The Irish writer Seán O'Casey comes closer to the truth about ravens and about corvids in general, in his book *The Green Crow*, when he writes that "Corvie is a gay chap for all his inky cloak." Quite right, Mr. O'Casey.

Some writers are genuine corvid enthusiasts. I've hosted a fair few of them in the Tower during my time here, all of them researching ravens for one reason or another, and I've always been amazed by their knowledge of and fascination with the birds. George R. R. Martin is one such writer. When I showed him around the Tower, he was keen to spend as much time with the ravens as possible, though all resemblances between our birds and the ravens in *Game of Thrones*, I should say, are entirely coincidental. In particular, since visitors to the Tower often ask, our birds *do not* have three eyes, and no, I've never seen one who does. And no, they *do not* deliver messages.

Lots of writers have kept corvids as pets and companions. Lord Byron kept a tame crow, I believe, though in fairness he also kept dogs, monkeys, peacocks, hens, an eagle, and a bear. The poet John Clare kept a raven, as did the American writer Truman Capote, whose raven was called Lola. Capote wrote about Lola in some detail in an essay first published in 1965, claiming that she used to cache various items in his bookcase behind *The Complete Jane Austen*, including a "purloined denture [. . .] the long-lost keys to my car [. . .] a mass of paper money [. . .] old letters, my best cuff links, rubber bands, yards of string" and "the first page of a short story I'd stopped writing because I couldn't find the first page." This all sounds rather unlikely to me, since our ravens in the Tower mostly tend to cache mice and bits of rat, but Mr. Capote was clearly a highly literary man with a highly literary raven. Either that, or he was making it up.

But it was of course *the* London writer, Charles Dickens, who kept the most famous ravens of all. Dickens mentions the Tower quite a few times in his novels. The Quilps in *The Old Curiosity Shop* live on Tower Hill. David Copperfield brings Peggotty to the Tower for a tour. And in *Great Expectations* Pip and Herbert row Magwitch past the Tower on their ill-fated trip down the Thames. I'll confess that this is where my wider knowledge of the work of Dickens ends—though when it comes to ravens, I can categorically state that he knew his birds.

The story of Dickens's ravens is well-known. In January 1841 the great man wrote to a friend about the new novel that he was working on. His big idea, Dickens wrote, was to have his main character "always in company with a pet raven, who is immeasurably more knowing than himself. To this end I have been studying my bird, and think I could make a very queer character of him." And a very queer character he makes of him indeed in *Barnaby Rudge*, his fifth novel, which is set during the anti-Catholic Gordon Riots of 1780, and in which the eponymous hero has a raven named Grip who accompanies him everywhere he goes. (Here at the Tower our Gripps have always had an extra "p" for reasons not entirely clear, though I suspect a clerical error.)

I may have a rather partial view, but to my mind Dickens counts as a genius not because of his prolific output, nor because of his famous public performances and his great public works, but because he gets every detail about ravens correct! He describes Grip's voice as being "so hoarse and distant, that it seemed to come through his thick feathers rather than out of his mouth," which is *exactly* where a raven's voice seems to come from. And the way he describes Grip's walk—well, that's the way our Gripp walks today! How did Dickens get it so right when so many other writers seem to get it so wrong, or simply see the ravens as symbols?

He lived with the birds, that's how. He observed them. He spent time with them. As he explained in the preface to *Barnaby Rudge*, "The raven in this story is a compound of two great originals, of whom I was, at different times, the proud possessor." Scholars believe that during his lifetime Dickens in fact kept three or four ravens, the first of whom, Grip, liked to nip the ankles of Dickens's children, whereupon he was barred from the house and banished outside. Unfortunately, just a few weeks after Dickens wrote about his idea of putting a raven in a novel, Grip died, as a result of having drunk or eaten some lead paint.

Dickens replaced Grip with two new birds: a second raven, also called Grip, and an eagle. The second Grip, according to Dickens's eldest daughter, Mamie, was "mischievous and impudent" and was eventually succeeded by a third Grip, who was so dominating that the family's large mastiff, Turk, even allowed him to eat from his bowl.

A true measure of Dickens's affection for the first Grip is that he had him stuffed and mounted in a case which he kept above his desk. (Actually, Dickens made a bit of a habit of stuffing his dead pets. When his cat Bob died, for example, he had one of his paws made into a letter opener.) After Dickens's death in 1870, a sale was held of his effects and the stuffed Grip eventually made it to America, where he can be seen in the Free Library in Philadelphia. A trip to see Grip in Philadelphia is another one of those adventures I've promised myself one day, though we do in fact have a perfectly good stuffed raven of our own here at the Tower. We have a little private museum on the ground floor of the Queen's House, which is not open to the public, but in there you'll find a rather handsome stuffed raven standing to attention on a perch in a very fine carved wooden case. A plaque on the case reads, "Black Jack, whose death was occasioned by the fearful sound of cannon upon the funeral of H. G. (His Grace) the Duke of Wellington, late Constable of the Tower of London, anno 1852." Some people have suggested that Black Jack may himself have been one of Dickens's birds, but I have seen no conclusive proof. What I do know is that several of the Tower ravens have been named in honor of Dickens's raven, as is our current Gripp, and that one of Gripp's earlier namesakes was resident during World War Two, he and his mate Mabel and another raven named Pauline being the only ravens to survive the Luftwaffe's bombing of the Tower, though alas, the Tower records suggest that after surviving the war, Pauline was killed by Mabel and Gripp. A truly tragic Tower tale.

Of course, the influence of Dickens's Grip goes way beyond the naming of our birds. Dickens was a great celebrity, and a bit like celebrities today with their shar-peis and French bulldogs, he helped set a trend. Thanks to Dickens and Grip, ravens became fashionable—maybe that's where the Yeoman Warders got the idea of importing a few tame ravens into the Tower in the 1880s? I offer this idea as a fruitful area of research to any corvidologists and Dickensians out there.

If Dickens was responsible for the interest in ravens in Britain—just as he's supposed to have invented the modern Christmas—it was Edgar Allan Poe who brought the birds to prominence in America.

Poe's poem "The Raven" caused something of a sensation when it was first published in 1845. According to one of his biographers, it is "the most popular lyric poem in the world." It's certainly well-known around the world: it even features in an episode of *The Simpsons*, which really does prove its canonical status.

Interestingly, Poe came to his raven through Dickens. In 1841 Poe was living in Philadelphia and was the editor of *Graham's Lady's and Gentleman's Magazine*, in which Dickens's *Barnaby Rudge* was being serialized. Poe reviewed the novel favorably—describing the character of Grip as "intensely amusing"—and in fact he met Dickens himself during Dickens's six-month visit to the United States in 1842. I've not been able to find any direct evidence of Poe's indebtedness to Dickens's Grip and *Barnaby Rudge*, but most Poe scholars seem to be in agreement that Poe was inspired by the book to produce his own famous tale of a talking raven in which "Once upon a midnight dreary," a forlorn student is thinking about his lost love Lenore. In Poe's poem, the student opens his window when he hears a tapping outside and a raven enters his room, perches upon a bust of Pallas, and when asked "Tell me what thy lordly name is on the Night's Plutonian shore!" the raven replies, rather enigmatically, "Nevermore," a word which he repeats in response to every one of the student's questions. In his dialogue with the raven, the forlorn lover begins to despair. Can I recite the poem? Absolutely! Have I taught the ravens to say "Nevermore"? Absolutely not.

Poe explained the rationale for his poem in his essay on "The Philosophy of Composition":

I had now gone so far as the conception of a Raven—
the bird of ill omen—monotonously repeating the one
word, "Nevermore," at the conclusion of each stanza,
in a poem of melancholy tone, and in length about
one hundred lines. Now, never losing sight of the object *supremeness*, or perfection, at all points, I asked
myself—"Of all melancholy topics, what, according
to the *universal* understanding of mankind, is the
most melancholy?" Death—was the obvious reply.
"And when," I said, "is this most melancholy of topics
most poetical?" From what I have already explained
at some length, the answer, here also, is obvious:
"When it most closely allies itself to *Beauty:* the death,
then, of a beautiful woman is, unquestionably, the
most poetical topic in the world—and equally is it
beyond doubt that the lips best suited for such topic
are those of a bereaved lover."

All of which brings us inevitably to the melancholy topic
of ravens and death.

24

DEATH AND THE RAVEN

Some people have a morbid fascination with ravens. I can understand why. They've been associated throughout history with death and doom and all things related to what the poet John Milton calls the "raven-down / Of darkness." As you probably know, collective nouns for a group of ravens include an "unkindness" and a "conspiracy." When humans were hunters, ravens were our companions—they came with us to find food and they were always there when there was food to be found, so right from the start of our culture they've been closely identified with hunting and with killing. It may be no coincidence then that I have spent so much of my life with ravens and feel comfortable around them: they are the soldier's natural ally. There's the story told by the Roman historian Livy, of Marcus Valerius fighting a giant Gaul—a real David and Goliath–type story—in which a raven assists the brave Valerius, who subsequently becomes known as Valerius Corvus. In the ancient Persian religion of Zoroastrianism, the raven was believed to be the incarnation of Verethragna, the god of victorious battles, and in the Mabinogion, the great Welsh collection of medieval tales about the ancient Britons, there's a story about the chieftains Arthur and Owein battling against each other, Owein with a band of magical ravens. And of course the Viking chiefs would go into battle bearing their raven standards. I think Skaife is a Viking name, by the way, so Chris "Corvus" Skaife . . . what do you think? It's got a ring to it, hasn't it?

Brave, ruthless, at home in war, and equipped with their own natural weapon—a bill as good as any axe or razor—ravens were renowned for following soldiers into battle in anticipation of rich pickings on the battlefield. They're omnivores, remember: they eat anything, and I mean *anything*. In the memorable words of Reginald Bosworth Smith in *Bird Life and Bird Lore*, their diet ranges "from a worm to a whale"—but they are particularly fond of carrion, including human carrion. (Execution sites in Britain were often known as the "ravenstone"—there's one up round Smithfield Market, where I go to collect meat for the birds.) Their reputation for feasting on flesh was soon matched by a reputation for feasting on souls: people used to say that ravens would sit on the roof of a house of the dead and the dying and wait for the soul to come up the chimney so they could gobble it down. It's ironic that I spend so much time feeding them, because rather more often they have fed on us!

It's perhaps no surprise, then, given their association with death and suffering, that the ravens are an important part of the tragic stories we tell at the Tower—including the tale of the last execution ever to take place here.

On the night of January 31, 1941, a man named Josef Jakobs parachuted out of a German plane and into the cold, quiet countryside of Ramsey Hollow in rural Huntingdonshire. Unfortunately for him, he broke his ankle on landing. Realizing that he couldn't continue with his mission, he fired two shots in the air with his pistol in the hope that it would attract attention—which it certainly did. Two farmers found him while out walking their dogs and alerted the police, whereupon it was discovered that Mr. Jakobs had in his possession a radio, maps, a large quantity of cash, and a codebook which he had attempted to destroy. He was put on trial at the beginning of August 1941. The charge was simple: "Committing treachery, in that you at Ramsey in Huntingdonshire on the night of 31 January 1941/1 February 1941 descended by parachute with intent to help the enemy." He was swiftly convicted of being a Nazi spy and was sentenced to death by firing squad. The death warrant was passed to the Constable of the Tower:

LD/SR A(s) 1 MOST SECRET
To: The Constable of H.M. Tower of London.
13th August 1941.

Sir,

I have the honour to acquaint you that JOSEF JAKOBS, an enemy alien, has been found guilty of an offence against the Treachery Act 1940 and has been sentenced to suffer death by being shot.

The said enemy alien has been attached to the Holding Battalion, Scots Guards for the purpose of punishment and the execution has been fixed to take place at H.M. Tower of London on Friday the 15th August 1941 at 7.15am.

Sgd. Sir Bertram N. Sergison-Brooke,
Lieutenant-General Commanding London District.

According to legend, just before the condemned man was escorted to his fate on the rifle range in the Casemates, just a few yards from my little house, a raven hopped down from Tower Green and stood croaking at the assembled execution-ers. An officer tried his best to drive the raven away but to no avail. Jakobs was blindfolded and the officer gave a silent sig-nal to the firing squad. It was not until the body was removed to the Tower morgue that the raven returned to his compan-ions on Tower Green.

There are all sorts of stories about the ravens of the Tower having an uncanny knowledge of impending death or disas-ter. Only recently one of our Tower residents told me that he was out watering his pot plants when Merlina perched on a post outside his house and croaked at him continually, some-thing she had never ever done before. He wondered if Mer-lina somehow knew that he had recently been seriously ill.

Stories about death and doom and ravens are one thing.

Stories about the death *of* ravens, well, they're another thing entirely and are much more difficult to tell. Before I go on, and before you judge me, I should point out that it's not uncommon for humans to grieve over birds, just as we grieve over any other animals. Mozart kept a starling, for example, which he named Star, which he bought for thirty-four kreuzer, from a shop in Vienna in 1784: the bird could sing the opening theme from the finale of his Piano Concerto no. 17 in G major, K453. When Star died, Mozart gave him a proper funeral and wrote an elegy in his memory. I'm no Mozart, but like all of the Ravenmasters, I certainly know what it's like to lose a bird.

Presented to the Tower in November 1995, Raven Thor was already four and a half years old on arrival, well into adulthood. We normally allow new ravens time to settle in before we release them to roam around the grounds, so Thor was kept in the hospital cage for a month while he adjusted to the surrounding area, the noise, and most important, the other ravens. He'd obviously been "humanized" and was used to socializing with people before being presented to the Tower. His human vocalizations were particularly good and he liked to greet everybody with a hearty "Good morning," much to the amusement of visitors and unsuspecting members of staff. He was such a friendly bird. It was Thor who was perched on the wooden steps leading up to the White Tower on the occasion of the official visit by Vladimir Putin and who greeted Putin with his deep bass "Good morning." He'd say hello to anybody, Thor.

Once he'd settled in, Thor liked nothing better than to spend his days hanging around on Tower Green, occasionally interacting with the other ravens, but generally keeping to himself. He made absolutely no effort to find a partner until one fine autumn morning he was spotted up close and personal with Munin. First Munin fanned out her tail. Then she fluffed up her feathers. And then she bowed her head in the traditional raven courtship ritual. She gave the distinctive knocking sound that female ravens like to make during courtship—and boom! She had him in her clutches. Thor was putty in her talons. He immediately succumbed to her advances and they became an item, preening and croaking to each other all day long. It was love at first peck.

At the time I was an assistant to the Ravenmaster Rocky Stones. One day I was on duty, getting the ravens up, feeding them, letting them roam free. I can tell you the exact date: February 6, 2010. A Saturday. Nothing out of the ordinary.

I remember clearly that Thor and Munin spent the day exploring the scaffolding that had recently been erected on the west side of the White Tower. Workmen had placed large wooden boards at the base of the scaffolding to stop the birds from getting in. The boards were painted gray to blend in with the surrounding stone walls. Elsewhere, fine netting was cable-tied to the poles, preventing the ravens from getting through the gaps and climbing up the scaffold. At least that was the idea. In practice it didn't work. I've seen ravens figure out entry and exit routes that you would simply never imagine a bird being able to work out. They are masters of escape and evasion. They'd do well on a Special Forces course. If a raven wants to get away, it will find a way.

I'd been working at my post for most of day when I realized that Munin and Thor had disappeared off my raven radar. Even though I couldn't see them, I somehow had a sense that they were no longer in the right place. Even back then I'd developed the habit of thinking about the birds all the time. Where are they? What are they up to? What have they eaten? Might they be injured? Are they okay? When people ask what it's like being the Ravenmaster I sometimes say that it's like going to a supermarket with seven young children, all of whom run off up and down the aisles in different directions. You have to be keyed up and switched on the whole time. You have to develop a sixth sense.

The Tower was about to close, so I decided to wait for lockdown before conducting a proper search. It would be much easier once the public had all departed—and you'd be surprised how quickly the duty supervisor and his Yeoman Warders can clear the Tower of visitors at the end of the day.

"All's-up!" came the call, which is the traditional signal to lift the drawbridges in preparation for our nighttime routine. It's our signal that the Tower is ours again.

And so I began my search for Munin and Thor.

Searching for the birds when they go missing is a bit like a game of hide-and-seek. Except you've got eighteen acres of the Tower to search. And you're looking for a creature that can fly. And blends into the shadows.

Half an hour passed and then an hour as I searched

everywhere in the Inner Ward, checking all the normal haunts. I tried everywhere, and eventually I had to admit defeat.

The light was fading. The Tower had fallen into its state of tranquility. The shouts and screams of excited children had disappeared, and the only sound that could be heard was the relentless hum of the city outside. I knew I didn't have long. If the ravens are left out at night in the dark, injured or feeding or simply resting at ground level, they're easy prey for the foxes.

I sat down heavily and waited, listening for any sign that would indicate where the birds could be. In the military we'd call it a combat indicator, something that stands out from the normal pattern, that doesn't quite fit, something that might reveal the whereabouts of your enemies.

You have to be careful, of course, when listening out for combat indicators: you can get it badly wrong. I can remember once when my team and I were tasked with conducting an overwatch on a muddy track in County Fermanagh that crossed the border between Northern Ireland and the Republic, a known crossing point used by the IRA to traffic weapons and explosives across the border at night. We'd selected a steep-sided hedge that gave us a bit of cover and protection from view, a typical Northern Irish hedge thick with brambles and foliage and with barbed wire twisted deep within. Getting over these sorts of hedges was affectionately known by us as the Fermanagh Wobble and it made getting into position particularly challenging. But eventually, under the cover of darkness, we clambered over, lay down, and began our watch.

It was pouring, as it always seemed to do when we were out on patrol. I swear even the clouds knew when it was time for us to leave base.

Hour after hour passed as we lay silently, listening to the sounds of the countryside. The world is strange at night. You start thinking dark thoughts. Then suddenly something stirred in the distance and we heard someone cough. This was it. Something was going down! There was another cough and then another. Someone was at the border crossing, waiting for an exchange of weapons. This was our time! We were about to foil an attack. We would catch an IRA cell. We would be heroes.

We called for backup and guided the satellite patrols toward the coughing.

Except there was no IRA cell exchanging weapons. We were not destined to become heroes. In fact, we were made to look like absolute fools. The coughing was coming from a herd of damned cows! At night a cow's cough can sound uncannily like a human's.

Lesson: Think before you act. A lesson we would all do well to learn.

I was looking up at the White Tower, hoping and praying that Munin and Thor hadn't found a way through the wooden panels and netting. I didn't fancy the climb up the scaffold steps in the twilight on the hunt for them. It had been a long day and I was looking forward to getting home and putting my feet up.

Was that them up there? I couldn't quite see.

It wouldn't have been the first time ravens had ventured up the scaffolding, and it certainly wouldn't be the last—the incident when I found myself dangling off the weathervane in pursuit of Munin was yet to come. I can well remember when I first started at the Tower, seeing one of the old assistants to the Ravenmaster swinging on the steel poles halfway up the Tower, on the hunt for one of the birds.

"All right?" I asked when he came down.

"Bloody ravens" is all he said in reply.

My instinct was telling me that the birds had found a way up and into the scaffolding. I concentrated, listening and watching. Nothing. If they were up there, they were in stealth mode, so I sat and waited.

•

It was no good. The rogue ravens were likely looking down at me sitting on the bench, laughing with one another. I would just have to flush them out. In the military we call this the clearance phase.

I made my way to the base of the White Tower and the temporary staircase that led to the roof. I took off my belt, my tunic, and my hat and placed them on a dusty workbench used for preparing the newly cut stone. And then I started my ascent up the steps that twisted and turned in a tight right-angled spiral all the way up the Tower. On each flight a wooden platform made of scaffold boards ran along the entire length of the Tower. I stopped at the first level and looked along it in the hopes that I would see or hear Munin and Thor. No sign of them.

Each flight of steps I climbed and each platform I checked took me nearer and nearer to the top, almost a hundred feet off the ground. I was about to make my last steps to the top platform when through a gap in the canvas hoarding I caught a glimpse of a dark wing and the unmistakable silhouette of a raven. Gotcha!

I had made contact with the "target" and my mission to bring them down was nearing completion. But I had no plan. Should I just race toward them, in the hope they would jump off and glide onto Tower Green one hundred feet below? Or should I sneak up on them both and attempt to catch them at the same time? If I just left them, maybe they would come down of their own accord? I decided to get a little closer.

I don't have many regrets in my life. I joined the military for fun and adventure but also because I believed I was serving Queen and country, and I was very proud to do so for the duration of my career. And since I became a Yeoman Warder, there's not a day that passes I'm not grateful: to me, it is the best job in the world. But things do go wrong, and with hindsight my presence up the White Tower, at dusk, on the hunt for two ravens was misjudged. To this day I wonder how I might have acted differently. But hindsight is a wonderful thing. What I think I learned is always to step back and consider my options more carefully, to slow down and think. If I'd simply waited a little longer, hunger would eventually have driven the ravens from their lookout position and back down to earth and everything would have been fine. I take full responsibility for the decision that I made at the time. I wasn't thinking like a raven.

I blame myself.

Munin jumped first. I couldn't see where she'd landed, but I knew she'd cleared the scaffolding and its hoardings and had reached Tower Green. She was safely down. And then Thor jumped—but Thor was a big bird, much bigger and heavier than Munin, and his wings had been trimmed just a few days before, which meant he couldn't gain momentum. He had bravely hopped and climbed and fluttered his way up the Tower, but a hundred-foot drop was another matter entirely. It was way beyond him, and I watched in horror as he jumped and began to plummet.

He didn't have a chance. Ravens are so intelligent. I'm sure Thor must have realized that he'd made a mistake. The dreadful thud as he hit the ground of the builder's yard below is something I will never forget—but worse was the silence that followed. For a moment I stood absolutely frozen, listening, hoping to hear him croaking once more his cheery "Good morning."

I raced down the scaffold steps and spotted him. He was on his back by the stonemasons' bench, his wings spread out, his head tilted to one side. I knew it was too late. I scooped him up and held him close to my chest. His eyes were still open and he looked at me for one last time before his life ebbed away.

I am not a sentimental man and I have seen much worse

in my military career, but I am not ashamed to admit that I shed a tear over Thor as he died in my arms that evening.

Ravenmaster Rocky Stones buried Raven Thor at 1755 hours on February 9, 2010, in a private burial. He then phoned Derrick Coyle, ex-Ravenmaster, who had cared for Thor for many years, to inform him of the sad loss. Colonel Dick Harrold, Deputy Governor to the Tower of London at the time, was informed the following morning of Thor's untimely demise and the circumstances surrounding his death. He immediately ordered that a complete review be conducted of the scaffolding on the White Tower and that further measures be put in place so that no other ravens would attempt the climb there again. The lesson was learned—by the Tower, and by me. Thor's death was one of the reasons I later changed our approach to feather trimming. As I explained, I now trim as little as possible, so that in the future a raven like Thor might stand a chance of surviving. His death was not in vain.

These days, if a raven dies unexpectedly at the Tower and I'm not sure of the cause of death, I take it to the vets at London Zoo for a postmortem. This allows us to rule out any possibility of a contagious illness that may have been passed on to any of the other ravens. (And it happens: in April 2010 we lost two ravens, Lizzie and Marley, from what we think was a viral infection, and it was only through our close observation and immediate action that we managed to save the other ravens from the same fate.)

If the cause of death is known to me, as in the sad case of

Thor, it's now my responsibility to ensure they are buried correctly within the grounds of the Tower. In the moat, by the Middle Drawbridge on the right-hand side as you exit the Tower, you will see a small black board with white letters painted on it. This is the Tower Ravens Memorial. The memorial board was erected by Henry Johns, Yeoman Quartermaster and keeper of the ravens for twenty-five years. It dates from 1956 and marks the deaths of all ravens who passed away at the Tower until 2006.

When I became Ravenmaster I decided not to continue updating the memorial. To me, what matters is the raven's life, not its death. All of my energies have been directed at ensuring that the birds have the best possible quality of life during their time with us. As the good book says, let the dead bury the dead.

The ravens who have passed away since I was appointed Ravenmaster have all received a quiet, simple burial within the grounds of the Tower. No official ceremony, just me and the raven, a time for me to say a private farewell and to thank the raven for its service to the Tower.

There is a curious coda to the story of Thor. After his death it didn't take long for the other ravens to realize Munin was now on her own and no longer a part of a dominant pair, so we moved her for her own protection away from the other ravens and put her in an enclosure next to Raven Gwylum.

Gwylum had arrived at the Tower in 1988 and at the time was one of our oldest ravens, age twenty-two, presented to the Tower by Mr. Jackson from the Welsh Mountain Zoo, Colwyn

Bay, North Wales. He was a quiet, unassuming raven who kept himself to himself and was perfectly happy with his own company, a confirmed bachelor—until, that is, Munin came along.

Almost instantly, through the cages they showed signs of courtship. Whether it was for comfort after the loss of Thor we shall never know, but one thing is for sure: Munin did not hang around before finding someone else. Maybe she had always had an eye for Gwylum and was waiting for the right moment. Thor died in February. By March we'd placed Munin and Gwylum in the same cage, where they showed signs of bonding, and by April we had returned them to the night box Munin had previously shared with Thor on Tower Green and they were released to continue life at the Tower as a newly bonded pair.

And then—unbelievably—history repeated itself.

On April 22, exactly a week after they'd been released, Munin took Gwylum with her to the top of the White Tower and wouldn't come down. We thought it was safe to go up again and flush them out: Gwylum's feathers had not recently been trimmed and we figured that both birds would be able to jump off and land safely without putting themselves in danger.

Once again I climbed the White Tower, and once again Munin leapt off and glided down to safety. I'll never forget the sight of Gwylum up on the parapet, moments before his leap: he hesitated, twitching his head nervously from side to side. I could see that he was calculating his options. Fight or flight? And then as I approached he tensed, sprang up, and launched himself off the White Tower.

"Rocky, Rocky! Did you see him?" I shouted down.

"I certainly did," Rocky replied, pointing toward the Thames. "He went thataway."

And that was the last time we ever saw Gwylum.

Within two and a half months Munin had inadvertently sealed the fate of two of our male ravens. Hence her nickname, the Black Widow. It wasn't until years later, in 2014, that she eventually found another, younger partner and bonded with Jubilee II. All I can do is wish him well.

25

THE GHOSTS OF MY LIFE

Some nights there are big events in the Tower. Corporate events. Clubs or societies visiting the Yeoman Warders Club. But not every night. Most nights it's just the Ceremony of the Keys—the ceremonial locking of the gates of the Tower—at 2200 hours. And then we Yeoman Warders have the place pretty much to ourselves.

People often ask if I believe in ghosts. To which the honest answer is yes. And no. You may remember that when Scrooge is confronted with the ghost of his business partner Jacob Marley in *A Christmas Carol* he says that he doesn't believe that he's a ghost: "You may be an undigested bit of beef, a blot of mustard, a crumb of cheese, a fragment of an underdone potato. There's more of gravy than of grave about you." I think at least some of our famous Yeoman Warder tales of ghosts and ghoulies have a touch more of the gravy than the grave about them. They're best taken with a large pinch of salt—and indeed a drop or two of whiskey, since they were most certainly concocted over a pint and a pie late at night in the Yeoman Warders Club. And yet . . .

I have to admit that there are some things about the Tower that one can't explain. You know me, I am an entirely rational rufty-tufty ex–infantry soldier, but even now, after almost fifteen years as a Yeoman Warder, wandering the Tower at night, even I can't help but half expect to meet Anne Boleyn or Sir Walter Raleigh or the two princes, or even just a headless soldier patrolling the battlements. Are there really such things as ghosts here, and do they stalk the ancient cobbles and passageways in the dead of night? I doubt it. But are there echoes of the past everywhere, shadows that beckon and call out to us, if only we'd pause and listen? Undoubtedly. The Tower is a place of memories and imaginings, an ancient site of banqueting and merrymaking, of coronations and carousing, of torture and of horror, and when the sun goes down and the shadows are low and distorted beyond all recognition by these cold stone walls, I would defy you not to begin to conjure up those memories and imaginings of a bloody and glorious past.

There have of course been many reported ghostly sightings here. One of our ex–Yeoman Warders, Geoffrey "Bud" Abbott, wrote a whole book about them. Bud was a great character and storyteller, and lots of us Yeoman Warders rely to this day on his accounts of ghouls and apparitions in *Ghosts of the Tower of London*. They're good stories. But because of the rather peculiar nature of my job, spending so much time wandering around the Tower alone late at night and early in the morning, I have experienced some uncanny goings-on firsthand.

I don't usually like to talk about these things, because frankly it can sound a bit crazy. Nonetheless, it's another necessary aspect of the Ravenmaster's work: coping with the ghoulies and ghosties and long-legged beasties and things that go bump in the night. Or at least the prospect of ghoulies and ghosties and long-legged beasties and things that go bump in the night. In Bud's words, "A candle flame is almost invisible in the sunlight—but it is still there. So it is with the Ghosts of the Tower of London—and if you look where the shadows linger, in the corners, round the stairs—you may see them too."

Our most famous resident ghost is Anne Boleyn. She's been spotted many times near the Queen's House and the Chapel of St. Peter ad Vincula on the anniversary of her death. I can remember when we first arrived at the Tower and my wife and I were living in a little flat on Tower Green. I awoke one early morning and felt compelled to look out of our bedroom window, only to see a distant shadow moving along the pathway that leads to the Chapel. Was it her? I don't know. It was certainly someone or something. Walter Raleigh was spotted as recently as 1976 by the wife of a Yeoman Warder while she was taking a bath. An unseen and terrifying presence is said to inhabit the Salt Tower after dark, and the ghost of a giant bear used to appear from inside the Martin Tower in the nineteenth century, apparently, though I don't know where he's got to recently. I can't verify or deny the truth of any of these sightings, but I can report on what I've seen and heard with my own eyes and ears.

A perfectly normal morning, a few years back: up before the alarm, cup of tea, out of the house, up the old spiral steps from the Casemates and onto Tower Green. Even before I see them or hear them I can sense the ravens itching to spread their wings and shake off the night's slumber. My radar's on: I know if anyone else is about and exactly what's happening.

The Tower clock was chiming from high above the entrance to the Jewel House. Six o'clock precisely, the sun low on the horizon, casting long shadows across the cobbled pathways that surround the Green. I walked across the grass, dodging the sprinklers, and made my way over to Merlina's night box.

I could hear her calling out to me. I'm sure she can sense my imminent arrival, just as I can sense her.

I opened the cage door, wished her good morning, as I do every morning, and off she went. She never hangs around once I open up. If she ever does, it's a good indication that something's not right. That morning she jumped off her perch and went flapping straight out onto the cobbled path. Sometimes, when it's pouring rain, she hesitates, as if to ask "Do I need an umbrella? What do you think?" But this morning, as usual, she unfolded her wings, shook them vigorously from side to side, dipped her head, raised her backside high in the air and proceeded to relieve herself right there in front of me. Her early morning ritual. Ravens, creatures of habit.

She hopped back onto the metal ladder, greeted me with a little bob of her head, half extended her wings, and gave out a loud belching croak. I returned the greeting. She then set off in the direction of her favorite holly tree next to the doctor's house, ready to hunt for a mouse. Merlina is an excellent mouser. (Her method is to hang around a hole, waiting for the mice to appear. It's easier that way. Mind you, I've also seen her take down a blue tit in full flight as it sped by her, so she's no slow-coach when it comes to hunting.)

I left her to her mousing and went to the little entrance by the Queen's House on Tower Green to get my broom and bucket in order to clear and fill the water bowls. It was a perfectly still morning. No one was around. I was completely alone. There was not a gust or a breeze. I walked a few feet toward the Green with my bucket and broom and the door to the entranceway suddenly slammed violently behind me, as if someone were furious or wanted to get my attention. I nearly leapt out of my skin. The door has never banged before or since, not once. I have no way of explaining why it happened.

Another story? Okay. Again, make of it what you will. And remember, at one time there may have been a strong motive for Yeoman Warders to invent stories, in order to encourage the visiting public to tip them generously, but this practice is now quite rightly discouraged, so there's no advantage to me whatsoever in concocting tales for you. I am simply reporting what I've seen.

One evening I was shepherding the ravens to bed. I unlocked the main enclosure door and went to round up Erin and Rocky. I could tell that they were keen to go to bed, but Erin has always had a habit of hesitating just before entering the enclosure, and as she did, I noticed a small girl sitting on the bench by the side of the enclosure, watching me closely.

She must have been about ten years old. No one was with her. She seemed to be on her own. She had mousy brown hair and was wearing normal modern clothes. I didn't recognize her as one of the residents' children and the Tower had long since shut, so she wasn't likely to be some stranded visitor. She sat perfectly still, in total silence, watching me.

I've often felt a bit uncomfortable in this area, but I try not to dwell on the matter. Unsure quite what to say, I asked the girl politely if she could move because the next couple of ravens would be unwilling to enter the enclosure if she didn't. She looked up at me and smiled slightly but still said nothing. I wondered perhaps if there was something wrong with her. Anyway, I had my job to do and I thought I'd deal with the ravens first, so I unlocked Munin and Jubilee's enclosure, which takes just a moment—a simple turn of a key—and when I turned back I saw that the young girl had disappeared. It would have been impossible for her to have walked past me without my noticing, but she was gone. Vanished. I was so unnerved by her sudden disappearance that I went to look for her, searching the entire Inner Ward. I found nothing, and to this day, though I've asked all the residents, no one knows anything about that little girl.

On another occasion, I remember the sun was shining brightly on Tower Green and the execution site. It seemed to wash away all traces of the Tower's bloody past. The compound was filled with the chatter of schoolchildren in their uniforms being led around by parents and teachers. I was on duty, enjoying the weather, watching Merlina playing with a stick. A girl broke away from her school group, came up to me, pointed toward the Beauchamp Tower, and told me there was a man in strange clothing walking around inside. She ran back to her school group. I thought no more of it—children's imaginations!—until later in the day when I suddenly remembered that some years before my wife had sensed something similar in Beauchamp Tower.

When I had applied to become a Yeoman Warder, but before my interview, we visited the Tower to explore our potential new home. Like all the other tourists, we took in all the sites and had a wonderful day. But as my wife walked through the doorway of Beauchamp Tower, she suddenly stopped and would go no farther. She became pale and seemed quite overcome. She could not bring herself to look around the lower floor and hurried out. Naturally, I followed her and asked if she was okay. She told me that as soon as she walked into the room she was overcome with a terrible feeling of dread, as if someone didn't want her to go any farther, as if she wasn't welcome there. She was really spooked.

Shortly afterward, when I had secured the job, the first house we were allocated was on Tower Green, next to the Bloody Tower and within sight of Beauchamp. For the whole time we lived on Tower Green, my wife never *ever* went near the Beauchamp Tower, and still refuses to do so today. She's not a superstitious person at all—she's not someone who'd jump at a shadow—but she is by no means the first person to sense something wrong there.

So no, I don't believe in ghosts. But I believe what I've seen and what people tell me. I believe that what we call ghosts might exist in our imaginations and that somehow, for some reason, we conjure them up when we are profoundly affected by our circumstances and our surroundings. Is that the ghost of Anne Boleyn? Are those the wraithlike figures of the boy princes? Or is it just you and your imagination?

26

AND SO TO BED

You can't just call a raven to bed. I mean, that would be ridiculous, right?

Right.

So I've had to develop a few strategies and methods.

I bang my stick and *then* I call them to bed.

You don't believe me? Well, let's just see, shall we. I'll get
the stick. It's a special raven-calling stick that I had made for
me by a long-lost raven-worshipping tribe over in South
America. Alas, no, it's not. I used to use a shepherd's crook, but
I'll admit that was a bit of a pose. Now I just use an old broom
handle. It does the job.

But first I need to check the water in the water bowls.
Make sure there's no debris lying around. Tidy up the remains
of any pigeon strikes.

Ravens normally sleep during the hours of darkness, and
although they don't actually tuck their head under their wing,
they do shut both eyes and nestle down. Our ravens normally

signal to me when it's time for bed by heading off to their favorite nighttime positions around the Tower and falling
silent. I can sense when they're ready.

Anyway. Here's the stick. I use it partly to guide the ravens toward their cages, but really it's to stop me falling over
on the Tower's often slippery and uneven ground. Walking
around in the dark, whistling and calling while guiding ravens in the general direction of the enclosure can be more difficult than it sounds. I've had enough trips and falls to last
me a lifetime—and I thought being an infantry soldier was
dangerous!

Do you remember I told you that when we release the
birds in the morning we have to do it in a particular order?
Well, they like to go bed in the same way every night, without exception, except in reverse: the system requires that the
dominant raven pair go to bed first, followed by the others.
There can be *no* deviation from this rule. This is one of the
Ravenmaster's Rules, remember?

And do you also remember that I said that sometimes
even I don't follow my rules? Well . . .

This was a few years ago. December. It was my birthday.
My wife and I had booked a restaurant not far from the
Tower. My wife was all ready to go and looking wonderful,
as usual. I, on the other hand, prefer to leave getting ready to
go out until the last possible moment. Dressing up smart re-
minds me too much of work. I've spent my whole life in uniform, so I tend to make the most of every moment when I can
be wearing just my T-shirt, my jeans, and my favorite Raven-
claw beanie. I had plenty of time.

The evening was particularly cold and miserable. There was that persistent light English drizzle that soaks you to the skin. I peered out of my living room window at the dark gray stone walls. The light was fading fast. It was still a little early to put the birds to bed, but I decided it would probably be fine just once to hurry them along.

•

I put on my waterproof jacket and my Wellingtons and my beanie and let my wife know that I was off to do the ravens: it's reassuring to know that on dark, wet nights, somebody knows where you are. Normally I take my phone with me, just in case. On this occasion I didn't.

This was only my second or third year as Ravenmaster and it had been a difficult time. I was on what you might call a steep learning curve. This was soon after a fox had killed two of the ravens. I just wanted the year to be over and to be able to start afresh.

I walked the short distance from our house in the Casemates onto Tower Green. Darkness had only just started to engulf the White Tower, casting sinister shadows down below. It would only be a matter of time before the Tower foxes came out to play.

I had a glance around. Merlina was nowhere to be seen, but that wasn't unusual. So I thought, I'll go and put the other ravens to bed first, then come back and look for her. It was important not to let Merlina know I was on a deadline. She's extremely smart and perceptive, as you know, and if you're stressed out, she senses it and refuses to come near you. A bit like an old dowager duchess, she does not like emotional displays of any kind. She finds too much enthusiasm or passion a real turnoff. At the slightest hint of emotion she will fluff her feathers at you, strut around in circles, cronk at you in disapproval, and then walk off until you calm down. Sometimes I wonder if she is the reincarnated spirit of Queen Victoria, or if she's been watching too much Dame Maggie Smith in *Downton Abbey*.

·

"I'll be back for you shortly, Merlina," I muttered into the night air, walking back toward the old night boxes.

And how convenient! Munin and Jubilee were right there waiting for me. Munin was pacing up and down a nearby grassy bank. She didn't like being out in the dark and preferred the security of Night Box 5, which is where they both slept before the new enclosure. Jubilee was standing on the ancient, dilapidated Cold Harbour wall, one of the ancient walls of the Tower, waiting patiently to follow Munin in. They were ready for bed.

The only problem was that Munin and Jubilee weren't supposed to go in first. They were the second mated pair in the pecking order. If you want to keep a raven as a pet—though I would strongly, strongly advise against it, don't even think about it—you could keep them wherever it is you choose for twenty years or more and they would be quite happy to stay there. I know people who've kept ravens in their houses. The moment you change something, anything, all hell is going to break loose. I know this. Everyone who works with ravens knows this. Never mess with the raven routine. But that night, I was foolish. I broke my own rules. I steered Munin and Jubilee into their night box. Great! I was two ravens down. I was on a roll.

Fool.

Next I went to get Erin and Rocky. As the dominant pair, they should have been the first two to go to bed. But I was sure they'd forgive me. It was my birthday, after all. And my wife was waiting for me. We had a table booked. I'd had a long and difficult year. Come on, guys, give me a break. This is why anthropomorphizing gets you into trouble: because ravens really don't care about your dinner plans.

I walked up the steep, wet, grassy bank on the Tower's south lawn, where Erin and Rocky would ordinarily be waiting for me, only to discover that they'd walked off in a huff, having being passed over for their normal bedtime privileges. They'd hopped up onto the wooden steps that lead to the southern entrance of the White Tower and were perched as high as they could possibly get, looking down at me from inside the steps, on one of the huge oak beams.

I checked my watch. Time was ticking on. My wife was waiting. So up I went. I was younger then and would often climb the beams under the White Tower steps in order to rustle the ravens down from their roost. This was going to be easy. Not a problem. First I tapped at the beams with my shepherd's crook, hoping that would encourage them down, but they refused to budge. Erin just shuffled along the beam farther away, closely followed by Rocky. Fine. I went straight after them, in almost total darkness, climbing up on the beams one by one. In moments I had them within touching distance.

Which is when my foot slipped on the slick ancient wood and I crash-landed, crotch first, onto a fat oak beam, which was better than falling and smashing my head open, obviously, but I can recall the excruciating pain even to this day. I did not move for a long time, for fear of further damaging my delicate parts.

Cronk. Cronk. I looked up and I swear to you, Erin and Rocky were laughing at me. Regaining my balance, I pulled myself up once more and started climbing again, cursing the day I decided it would be fun to be the Ravenmaster.

When I finally made it to the beam Erin and Rocky were perched on, I was actually rather proud of myself for climbing up in the dark, despite being injured.

"Come on, you two, off you come," I said, tapping the beam gently with my crook, which I still held firmly in my hand.

Erin and Rocky took one look at me, and like BASE jumpers throwing themselves from the highest clifftop, they jumped off into complete darkness.

By the time I was back on terra firma, they had sauntered into their home, Night Box 4. I wished them good night, cursed them under my breath and shut the night box door behind them—rather harder, I confess, than I should have.

Right. Four ravens down, three remaining! I opened Night Box 3 for Porsha and Night Box 1 for Hugine. Porsha and Hugine were females and preferred to go to bed separately. These two never normally gave me the runaround. But now everything and everyone was out of sync and I was beginning to feel the pressure.

Fortunately for me, though, Porsha and Hugine were as good as gold that night. They both hadn't yet established themselves within the hierarchical order, so it didn't matter to them so much about the upset in the usual bedtime rituals and routines.

Hugine was hanging out on the west side of the White Tower, while Porsha was standing on the Maltese Cannon over on the east side of the Tower. God bless her, as soon as she saw me, Hugine glided down to her night box, went straight in, and I shut the door behind her. Wonderful! What a beautiful raven she was, and so obedient! It was looking like my birthday celebrations might be back on track. Porsha followed suit. She was a raven who liked her own company and didn't really socialize with any of the other ravens, choosing to spend her time posing for photographs on top of the cannon. She always did a lap of honor of the south lawn before going into her night box, and this evening was no different. Straight off the cannon, one lap around the lawn, and home to bed!

So, all ravens to bed on the south lawn area. I secured the outer cage door, wished the ravens good night and walked away.

•

Only one more raven remained: the dowager duchess herself, Merlina.

Darkness now completely enveloped the Tower. I stood in the center of Tower Green and called out in Ravenish.

Merlina didn't reply. I checked my watch again. My wife would now be standing by our front door.

I hurried off to look for Merlina in her favorite places, to see if she was playing hide-and-seek, as she likes to do when she wants to hold me up. First I searched the holly tree. No sign of her. Then I searched both Christmas trees on Tower Green—I'd seen her climb up the center of the trees a number of times during December and pop the lightbulbs using her beak. Again, nothing.

I widened my search and climbed the steps of the Bloody Tower to see if she was perched on the top of Raleigh's Walk. She liked to look over at the boats going up and down the Thames. No doubt Sir Walter Raleigh did exactly the same thing four hundred years earlier during his imprisonment in the Tower. But Merlina wasn't up on the wall. I came down the steps a bit sharpish. I've never felt entirely comfortable on Sir Walter's walkway. Something about it always makes me feel sad.

Anyway, time was getting on. At this rate, I was going to miss my birthday meal. And worse, I was keeping my wife waiting. I would have to go to DEFCON 2. I hurried to the storeroom to get out the shark's eye—in the army that's what we call a bright searchlight. If Merlina was hiding in some dark recess, the shark's eye would soon flush her out.

I walked around the Inner Ward again, shining the shark's eye. Nothing. Our table was booked for 2100. I now had less than one hour to find a raven, get ready for my night out, and get to the restaurant. Not absolutely impossible, but my window of opportunity was closing fast.

I walked under the archway of the Bloody Tower, up the cobbled incline toward Tower Green, when suddenly I heard a faint cronking sound. I stood motionless for a moment, straining to hear the noise again.

It must have been my imagination, so I carried on walking. But as I got to the boardwalk steps, I heard it again, only this time it was clear. *Kn-ck, kn-ck*, the distinctive clicking sound Merlina and I use to acknowledge each other. I couldn't make out where the sound was coming from, so I called back to see if she would answer. To my great relief she did. Fantastic! I had found her. It was a Christmas miracle!

The miracle was short-lived when I realized just where she was. She had managed to scramble under the wooden platform that leads into the lower chamber of the Wakefield Tower, where we keep our instruments of torture. There was a gap of all of about eight inches and Merlina had managed to cram herself in there.

I had no idea how I was going to get her out. The platform sits above a big stinking pit, about twenty feet in width and seven feet in depth. It was once the site of an old Georgian guardhouse, but it now has no function whatsoever, apart from collecting stagnant rainwater, tourist rubbish, and pigeon carcasses. I always refer to it as the Pit of Doom. It was now the only obstacle between me and my birthday celebrations.

I climbed over the black iron fence that wraps its way around the grassy areas of the Tower and got down onto my belly. The grass was soaking wet, but at this stage I didn't care. The insides of my legs were already painfully bruised from my unfortunate encounter with Erin and Rocky. I had walked what seemed like miles looking for Merlina, and I was soaked to the skin. What more could possibly go wrong?

I shone my shark's eye under the platform to see if indeed it was Merlina there and not the ghost of Christmas past, and called to her again. She didn't call back, but I could make out the silhouette of her beak, and that was good enough for me. She had tucked herself right at the very back of the tiny crack and was out of reach even with my crook at its fullest extent. I would have to venture into the Pit of Doom.

Wading into the seven-foot-deep pit was something I certainly didn't want to do, since I'm rather shorter than seven feet and had no desire to drop down into a well of filthy stagnant water. Fortunately there is a set of narrow steps attached to the wooden uprights that line the pit, presumably there for the maintenance boys to access the area. If I could just ease myself around the pit on the steps I'd be able to reach into the gap for Merlina.

I lowered myself onto the first step, putting my foot on it to see if it would take my weight. No problem. Second step, good, all okay. Third step: CRACK.

I had one of those life-flashing-before-your-eyes sorts of moments and the next thing I remember is sinking down into the stinking pool of water as rubbish and rotting pigeon carcasses swirled around me. I couldn't believe my luck, or lack of it. I dragged myself out of the stinking water, and as I did so, I made direct eye contact with Merlina, who had crawled out of her hiding place and was perched directly over me, wagging her beak.

I've seen it many times during my military career: when things just can't get any worse, for some reason you start to laugh. This was one of those moments.

We never got out for my birthday dinner. Fortunately my wife also saw the funny side of the story. We stayed in that night for a romantic meal of beans on toast for two.

That's another thing you definitely need as a Ravenmaster: a sense of humor. And a forgiving partner.

Now let me call the birds in—in the correct order. I'll bang the stick.

Erin and Rocky.

Harris and Gripp.

Munin and Jubilee.

That's the way to do it.

27

GREAT TRADITIONS

So the birds are back in their enclosure for the night, safe from the foxes, and I hope by now I've answered most of your questions. There is one important question, though, that people don't tend to ask, which I suppose is really only for me to ask: What's the future of the ravens at the Tower?

To be honest, it feels like I've only just begun with the work I want to do here. I've been able to make a lot of changes since I took over as Ravenmaster, with the full support and encouragement of the staff of Historic Royal Palaces, particularly in terms of how we care for the ravens. I believe the changes we've made have been absolutely necessary. Our visitors have greater levels of expectation than ever before, especially when it comes to the ravens' welfare, and these days we're all much more informed about how animals should be treated. I've been able to develop my own ideas about what I think we should do with the birds and I've been privileged to work with a brilliant team of assistants and volunteers to be able to make it happen.

Being in the army taught me to take responsibility. When I was young I was always in a gang, but I was always on the periphery. I enjoyed being part of the pack, but I also tended to hang back a bit and observe. I was reluctant to commit. But now I see the importance of making plans, working with your team to carry them through, and assessing the consequences. I can remember going back to my battalion to take over as Drum Major when I was in my early thirties and realizing I'd come full circle: twenty years after arriving as a boy soldier, I was running the platoon. Now, to be a Yeoman Warder, and also to be the Ravenmaster and a part of Team Raven, it's a great source of pride to me, as well as a great responsibility.

My primary job is to maintain the presence of the ravens at the Tower, ensuring there's no break in the tradition—which, as you now know, may or may not be a tradition entirely invented by my Victorian predecessors, but which is important nonetheless! I'm an ex-soldier and I work for Historic Royal Palaces at a World Heritage Site, so you'd expect me to be interested in upholding tradition. But change is inevitable. Even during my time in the British Army, a famously hidebound and slow-moving organization, there were in fact constant changes. When I first became a boy soldier, for example, we did our basic training at Bassingbourn Barracks in Cambridgeshire, which is the place where Stanley Kubrick filmed *Full Metal Jacket*, and certainly when I joined up, the film was a pretty accurate portrait of basic military training! Looking back now I find it amazing that any of us survived. But by the time I became an army instructor the whole approach had changed for the better.

I'm very fortunate that I've had my wife to support me in all the challenges in my life and career, right from the beginning, with every deployment and every difficult decision. I remember I was on a senior NCO course once and I just wanted to come off it and give up, so I rang home, and my wife told me to stick with it: I became a sergeant as a consequence. Even when I started as a Yeoman Warder, we'd been living in a big house in Brighton and we turned up at the Tower and we were given the keys to our first tiny flat next to the Bloody Tower and we couldn't even fit our sofa through the front door. Again I was ready to walk away, but my wife said fine, we'll just put everything we own into storage and then we'll arrange to have the windows taken out so we can get the furniture in, which is exactly what we did. Whoever you are, wherever you are, whatever you do in life, you have to learn to adapt.

I think what would be really interesting to do next at the Tower would be to establish a raven breeding program. Something similar has been tried before, and there have been ravens who were born here—Ronald Raven was the first, in 1989, and there were maybe a dozen others during the late 1980s and early 1990s—but there's never really been a properly organized and monitored program. One of my predecessors as Ravenmaster, the great John Wilmington (4th Queen's Own Hussars), made notes about his own struggle to encourage the birds to breed:

For many years I've tried to get them to mate and produce but to no avail. I've tried nests in the cage by Queen's House; I've tried them in the arrow slits by the Wakefield Tower; I've tried them beneath the stairs of the White Tower itself; and this was a partial success, for they built a splendid nest—I brought wood and things for them to help them on their way, and they produced two lovely eggs which went well, they took turn about in feeding, preening, looking after one another on the nest, for nine days and then for some unknown reason they destroyed the eggs, but talking to the experts, they tell me that this quite often happens.

Nothing worth doing is ever easy.

I would really love the public to be able to experience what I've been privileged to witness over the years—from egg to adulthood, the whole process. A baby raven looks a bit like a grotesque miniature gargoyle, but then you see them grow and develop and you see them washing themselves and feeding themselves, becoming fully alert as they crane their tiny necks. It really is wonderful: it's an education.

I think it would also be good to establish a breeding program here to enable us to get the right sort of birds into the Tower. As I said, at one time all our ravens were simply presented to us, often by old soldiers, or sometimes from zoos or indeed from members of the public who had just found ravens in the wild. I don't agree with bringing birds born in the wild into the Tower, and there just aren't that many breeders of captive ravens in the U.K., so we really do need to find our own solution if we're to continue with our tradition. Ravens are now reestablishing themselves throughout the U.K.— and have now settled within about a thirty-mile radius of London. Perhaps one day we'll even see wild ravens return to the Tower!

28

SENTINELS OF THE WHITE TOR

The old Ravenmasters liked to keep their knowledge to themselves. The care of the Tower ravens and the life of the Tower ravens was all a bit of a mystery. For better or for worse, I have taken the opposite approach. I suppose it's just who I am. The Ravenmasters in years to come will doubtless do things differently as well. Once there was the Keeper of the Lions and Leopards, then there was the Master of the King's Bears and Apes, then the Yeoman Quartermaster, and now there is the Ravenmaster. Who knows what the role will be in years to come?

At this stage in my career, I suppose I just wanted to share what I've learned about the birds from observing and working with them. I hope you've seen that, in a sense, caring for the ravens is easy, in the same way that caring for any animal is easy: you feed them, ensure they have enough water, keep them safe, and that's about it—that's all you really have to do. But fortunately, for most of us, thank goodness, caring isn't just about meeting another creature's basic needs. For me, after my life in the army, caring for the ravens has meant becoming a part of another family, of learning to trust and be trusted, of seeking to understand their needs, of being alongside them when they're happy or depressed, when they're angry or lonely, and of doing what I can, to the best of my ability, when they need my help.

If I had to sum up my raven care philosophy, it would be this: Animals are individuals just like us and they deserve to be treated with respect. A bit like a Yeoman Warder, the Tower ravens have a job to do: upholding tradition and reminding us of our past. In return, they get their food and lodgings for free. They rely on us, and we rely on them. And that's it.

If you are in any way interested in birds, and yet like me just a few years ago you don't know where to start, I suggest studying a particular bird: don't try to learn about every species all at once. Pick a bird you love, or which fascinates you in some way. It doesn't matter which one: a goose, a swan, a sparrow, a hawk. Learning about birds, like learning anything else, is all about patience and persistence and just doing the little things right, again and again. Get to know your bird. Attend to their peculiar traits and the shape of them, their flight, their song, the way they walk. Study their talons, their feathers, their tails. Look into their eyes.

Read a few books. Start with the easy stuff and then work up to the great scholars in the field: Bernd Heinrich, John and Colleen Marzluff, Oskar and Katharina Heinroth, Konrad

Lorenz, Eberhard Gwinner. Go slowly. Be inquisitive. Be curious.

And my final piece of advice is this: In the end, to understand birds, you've got to be able to think like a bird. Which sounds ridiculous. But I believe that with just a bit of effort and imagination it's possible at least to see things from their perspective, and so to begin to understand why they do what they do, how they feel, and why they are so similar and yet so utterly different from us.

•

Thank you so much for allowing me to share my love for the ravens of the Tower. Perhaps I might ask you to do me a small favor in return?

Years from now, long after our current ravens have gone, and I too have passed on to that great raven enclosure in the sky, you may be visiting the Tower. Perhaps there's a raven there called Skaife and he is looking at you in that way that only ravens can. Don't get too close—he may bite. But perhaps you might say hello to him from me.

Kn-ck, kn-ck. Kn-ck, kn-ck.

29

RISING ABOVE

Final check: 2300 hours.

Once again, it's just me and the birds. The Tower is in darkness. Everyone is asleep.

I rise up onto Tower Green and open up the night box for Merlina. She's the last to bed. She only goes to bed once all the other ravens have been put away for the night. Often she refuses to go to bed at all and stays up on the rooftops. It looks like she's going to stay there tonight, watching and thinking.

Almost a thousand years ago a great fortress was built by a river on its northern shoreline, on the site of an old Roman fort, a huge building reaching skyward, the likes of which no one in England had seen before. Designed to provide security and protection, it was also a reminder to the citizens of the city that they had been conquered.

Rising above it all were the birds.

They rise above it still.

APPENDIX
RAVENMASTERS SINCE 1946

Pre-1946 there is little or no evidence of particular Yeoman Warders being tasked to care for the ravens. It is assumed therefore that the task of caring for the birds either fell to the Yeoman Quartermaster or was left to the garrison soldiers to feed them under the supervision of the Yeoman Warders.

Yeoman Quartermaster*
Henry Thomas Johns, Regimental Sergeant Major (RSM)
Duke of Cornwall's Light Infantry (DCLI)
Yeoman Quartermaster, responsible for looking after the ravens
    1946–1969.
Yeoman Warder Number: 230
Enrolled 1946–1970

Raven Master
John Wilmington, British Empire Medal (BEM) Staff Sergeant
    Major (SSM)
4th Queen's Own Hussars / Queen's Royal Irish Hussars (QRIH)
Raven Master, 1969–1992
Yeoman Warder Number: 282
Enrolled 1968–1992

*Change from Yeoman Quartermaster to Raven Master officially by 1969.

Ravenmaster*
David Arthur Cope, Colour Sergeant (C/Sgt)
Royal Marines (RM)
Ravenmaster, 1992–2000
Yeoman Warder Number: 321
Enrolled 1982–2000

Ravenmaster
Derrick Coyle, Royal Victorian Medal (RVM) Regimental Sergeant Major (RSM)
Green Howards (GH)
Ravenmaster, 2000–2009
Yeoman Warder Number: 329
Enrolled 1984–2009

Ravenmaster
Ray (Rocky) Stones, Colour Sergeant (C/Sgt)
Scots Guards (SG) (band)
Ravenmaster, 2009–2011
Yeoman Warder Number: 368
Enrolled 2000–2011

Ravenmaster
Chris Skaife, Colour Sergeant (C/Sgt)
Queens Regiment / Princess of Wales's Royal Regiment (QR) (PWRR)
Ravenmaster, 2011–present
Yeoman Warder Number: 379
Enrolled 2005–

*Change from Raven Master to Ravenmaster over time due to misspelling.

SUGGESTED READING

ON RAVENS, BIRDS, AND OTHER CREATURES

Angell, Tony. *Ravens, Crows, Magpies and Jays*. Seattle: University of Washington Press, 1978.

Armstrong, Edward A. *The Folklore of Birds: An Enquiry into the Origin and Distribution of Some Magico-Religious Traditions*. London: Collins, 1958; 2nd ed., rev. & enl., Mineola, N.Y.: Dover Publications, 1970.

Bekoff, Mark. *Minding Animals: Awareness, Emotions, and Heart*. Oxford and New York: Oxford University Press, 2002.

Blunt, Wilfrid. *Linnaeus: The Compleat Naturalist*, rev. ed. Princeton: Princeton University Press, 2001.

Bonner, John Tyler. *The Evolution of Culture in Animals*. Princeton: Princeton University Press, 1980.

Capote, Truman. *A Capote Reader*. New York: Random House, 1987.

Dixon, Charles. *The Bird-Life of London*. London: William Heinemann, 1909.

Dolan, Edward F. *Animal Folklore: From Black Cats to White Horses*. New York: Ivy Books, 1992.

Emery, Nathan J. *Bird Brain: An Exploration of Avian Intelligence*. Princeton: Princeton University Press, 2016.

Feher-Elston, Catherine. *Ravensong: A Natural and Fabulous History of Ravens and Crows*. Flagstaff, Ariz.: Northland Publishing, 1991; repr. New York: Jeremy P. Tarcher / Penguin, 2005.

Fisher, James. *The Shell Bird Book*. London: Ebury Press and Michael Joseph, 1966.

Gill, Sam D., and Irene F. Sullivan. *Dictionary of Native American Mythology*. Oxford and New York: Oxford University Press, 1992.

Goodchild, Peter. *Raven Tales: Traditional Stories of Native Peoples*. Chicago: Chicago Review Press, 1991.

Goodwin, Derek. *Crows of the World*, 2nd ed. London: Natural History Museum Publications, 1986.

Heinrich, Bernd. *Mind of the Raven: Investigations and Adventures with Wolf-Birds*. New York: Cliff Street Books / HarperCollins, 1991.

————. *Ravens in Winter*. New York: Summit Books, 1989.

Hudson, W. H. *Birds and Man*, rev. ed. London: Duckworth & Co., 1915.

Lawrence, R. D. *In Praise of Wolves*. New York: Henry Holt, 1986.

Leeming, David Adams, with Margaret Adams Leeming. *A Dictionary of Creation Myths*. Oxford and New York: Oxford University Press, 1994.

Lorenz, Konrad. *King Solomon's Ring: New Light on Animal Ways*. London: Methuen, 1952; repr. London, Routledge Classics, 2002.

Marzluff, John M., and Tony Angell. *In the Company of Crows and Ravens*. New Haven, Conn.: Yale University Press, 2005.

O'Casey, Seán. *The Green Crow*. New York: George Braziller, 1956.

Ratcliffe, Derek. *The Raven: A Natural History in Britain and Ireland*. London: T and AD Poyser Ltd., 1997.

Ritvo, Harriet. *The Animal Estate: The English and Other Creatures in the Victorian Age*. Cambridge, Mass.: Harvard University Press, 1989.

Rothenberg, David. *Why Birds Sing: A Journey into the Mystery of Bird Song*. New York: Basic Books, 2005.

Rowland, Beryl. *Birds with Human Souls: A Guide to Bird Symbolism*. Knoxville: University of Tennessee Press, 1978.

Savage, Candace. *Bird Brains: The Intelligence of Crows, Ravens, Magpies, and Jays*. San Francisco: Sierra Club Books, 1995.

Sax, Boria. *City of Ravens*. London and New York: Duckworth Overlook, 2011.

Swainson, Charles. *The Folk Lore and Provincial Names of British Birds*. London: Elliot Stock, 1886.

Turville-Petre, E.O.G. *Myth and Religion of the North: The Religion of*

Ancient Scandinavia. New York: Holt, Rinehart and Winston, 1964.

Wilmore, Sylvia Bruce. *Crows, Jays, Ravens and Their Relatives*. Exeter, Devon, U.K.: David and Charles, 1977.

Woolfson, Esther, *Corvus: A Life with Birds*. London: Granta Books, 2008; Berkeley, Calif.: Counterpoint, 2009.

ON THE TOWER OF LONDON, ENGLAND, AND FOLKLORE

Abbott, Geoffrey. *Mysteries of the Tower of London*. Nelson, Lancashire, U.K.: Hendon Publishing, 1998.

Ackroyd, Peter. *Albion: The Origins of the English Imagination*. London: Chatto and Windus, 2002; New York: Nan A. Talese / Doubleday, 2003.

Bell, W. G. *The Tower of London*. London: Lane, 1921.

Benham, William. *The Tower of London*. London: Seeley and Co., 1906.

Borman, Tracy. *The Story of the Tower of London*. London: Merrell Publishers in association with Historic Royal Palaces, 2015.

Brooke-Hunt, Violet. *Prisoners of the Tower: Being an Account of some who at divers times lay captive within its walls*. London: Dent, 1899.

Dixon, William H. *Her Majesty's Tower*, 7th ed. 2 vols. New York: Thomas Y. Crowell, 1884. Orig. pub. 1869.

Hahn, Daniel. *The Tower Menagerie: Being the Amazing True Story of the Royal Collection of Wild and Ferocious Beasts*. New York: Simon & Schuster, 2003.

Harper, C. G. *The Tower of London: Fortress, Palace and Prison*. London: Chapman and Hall, 1909.

Impey, Edward, and Geoffrey Parnell. *The Tower of London: The Official Illustrated History*. London: Merrell Publishers, 2000.

Leigh, Felix. *London Town*. London: Marcus Ward, 1883.

Loftie, W. J. *Authorized Guide to the Tower of London*. London: H. M. Stationery Office, 1888.

Mears, Kenneth J. *The Tower of London: 900 Years of English History*. London: Phaidon, 1988.

Murphy, Clare, and David Souden, eds. *Prisoners of the Tower: The Tower of London as a State Prison, 1110–1941*. Hampton Court Palace, Surrey, U.K.: Historic Royal Palaces, 2004.

Newbery, Elizabeth. *Tower Power: Tales from the Tower of London*. Hampton Court Palace, Surrey, U.K.: Historic Royal Palaces, 2004.

Rowse, A. L. *The Tower of London in the History of England*. New York: Putnam, 1972.

Westwood, Jennifer, and Jacqueline Simpson. *The Lore of the Land: A Guide to England's Legends, from Spring-Heeled Jack to the Witches of Warboys*. London: Penguin, 2005.

Wilson, Derek. *The Tower of London: A Thousand Years*, 2nd rev. ed. London: Allison and Busby, 1998. Orig. pub. 1978.

Younghusband, George. *A Short History of the Tower of London*. London: Herbert Jenkins, 1926.

———. *The Tower from Within*. London: Herbert Jenkins, 1918.

ACKNOWLEDGMENTS

Little did I know as I sat one balmy evening in the Yeoman Warders Club having a few drinks with friends that it would lead me on such an epic journey into the labyrinth of publishing. This book has been a labor of love and I have seen my fair share of highs and lows.

So before I start thanking the amazing people who have been with me throughout this journey, I have two very special people in my life without whose love and support this book would undoubtedly still only be a dream.

Jasmin, thank you for all your love, support, and cake! You are my world, without you I am nothing. I love you, xxx.

Mickayla, you will always be my little girl, you are beautiful in every way and I'm so proud of you. I love you, xxx.

•

Who would have ever thought when I was a young boy growing up in the sleepy backwaters of Dover that I would become the author of a book about the Tower of London's famous ravens? Certainly not my schoolteachers, or the policeman who grabbed me by the scruff of the collar and dragged me out of the old Ford Anglia car that I was about to drive off in!

Throughout life I have tried my very best to surround myself with people who say "Yes you can do it" rather than "No you can't." You have two choices: you can have a glass that is half full or a glass that is half empty. I prefer my glass full to the brim.

Talking about full glasses, I raise mine and want to say a huge thank-you to my good friends Lindsey Fitzharris and Adrian Teal, who have made me do endless tours around the Tower, meeting with absolutely anyone who would listen to us ranting on about our crazy ideas. They have forced me to drink copious amounts of gin (Beefeater, of course) and have always believed in me. CHEERS!

•

Sometimes we meet people who are destined to enrich and change our lives forever, and Devon Mazzone and the team at Farrar, Straus and Giroux are such people. Devon, thank you for being such a huge corvid fan and having the fore-sight and belief in me to tell my story about my beloved ravens.

Anna Sproul-Latimer at the Ross Yoon Agency, I dip my feathered hat to you for being my agent and taking on such a mammoth task. If you had wings you would be an angel, albeit a rather dark one! We have greatly appreciated your patience and guidance throughout.

Amanda Moon and Colin Dickerman, my editors at Farrar, Straus and Giroux, thank you so much for your hard work—you and your team are now part of Tower history. Ian Sansom, where are you, sir? Yes . . . I see you standing there, watching, and listening to my endless ramblings. Your patience and attention to detail is legendary. You are a true gentleman and a literary genius, and I can't thank you enough for bringing the story of the Tower Ravens to life.

John Brown and James Murly-Gotto at Historic Royal Palaces, I thank you. John, you were a great advocate for me and had the foresight to support me from the very start. James, you have been a constant throughout this process, and I thank you for the tremendous hard work you have done on my behalf, and I look forward to watching your children grow up around the ravens on Tower Green.

A huge thank-you must go to all the staff at Historic Royal Palaces, especially Catherine Steventon and Sarah Kilby for keeping me on the straight and narrow. And to "Team Raven," Shady, Barney, Mark, Steve, and Jase, who suffer my insanity every day. Also, thank you to the vets both past and present at the Zoological Society of London (ZSL) for the care you have given the ravens over the years.

I thank Dr. Nathan Emery for his love and dedication to corvids and for sending me his students from Queen Mary University of London. Boria Sax (*City of Ravens*), you were right! Thank you for your amazing contribution. Lori Burchill, thank you for your kindness and for welcoming Team Raven into your family. We miss Martin greatly and will take good care of Harris for you.

Thank you to all the social media followers who like, share, or comment on my posts on a daily basis, enjoying my raven photos, stories, and silly quips. The power of social media! Let's use it positively—it's much more fun!

Looking after the ravens of the Tower has been a constant part of my life since I took over as Ravenmaster, and as a result of that, they have provided me with enrichment and endless inspiration. But I have shared my passion with my family and friends, perhaps a little more than I should have! As the ravens have been a big part of my life, so have they been a big part of my family's life too.

I want to thank you all for putting up with my early mornings and late nights, chasing ravens and endlessly chatting about their antics, especially considering that most of you prefer power tools . . . Stuart!

Children teach us so much and the children in my life are absolutely no exception!

•

Flynn, thank you for listening to my endless childhood stories, even though your mum wasn't always best pleased about my more enlightening ones! Lottie, you always laugh at my silly jokes—you are a rare breed indeed! Thank you for humoring me. Fergus, we have watched you grow into a fine young man, feeding the ravens and experiencing "Tower Life"—thank you for letting me and the ravens be part of your childhood memories.

Little Charlie, never lose your love of the Tower and its

magnificent ravens. Your constant excitement when you visit us simply inspires me.

I have two young ladies in my life who visit me often. Nyah and Izzy can recite all the ravens' names and love to help me put the ravens to bed at night. They frequently ring me up asking for information on their next school project! This has given me endless joy and entertainment, so a big thank-you from "Christopher Robin," as they affectionately know me.

I want to thank all my friends who I have neglected throughout this whole process—you know who you are, and I promise I will be back in the land of the living soon . . . well, for a little while, at least.

And finally, I want to thank the ravens. They won't know, nor do I suspect they care, that they have unintentionally changed my life forever and filled it with joy. . . . I can ask for nothing more from them. A very special thank-you to Munin. During the publication of this book, sadly, Raven Munin passed away due to complications of old age. Her presence at the Tower will be greatly missed by her partner, Jubilee; by Team Raven; and by all staff at Historic Royal Palaces.

A NOTE ABOUT THE AUTHOR

Before becoming Yeoman Warder and Ravenmaster at the Tower of London, Christopher Skaife served in the British Army for twenty-four years, during which time he became a Drum Major as part of a specialist machine gun platoon. He has been featured on the BBC, the History Channel, PBS, *BuzzFeed*, *Slate*, and other media. He lives at the Tower with his wife, his daughter, and, of course, the ravens. Follow him on Twitter at @ravenmaster1.

PLEASE SHARE YOUR THOUGHTS
ON THIS BOOK

Comments:	Comments:
Humorous as Well as Informative	
Comments:	Comments:
Comments:	Comments:
Comments:	Comments:
Comments:	Comments:
Comments:	Comments:

6431

A True and Exact Draught of the TOWER LIBERTIES,

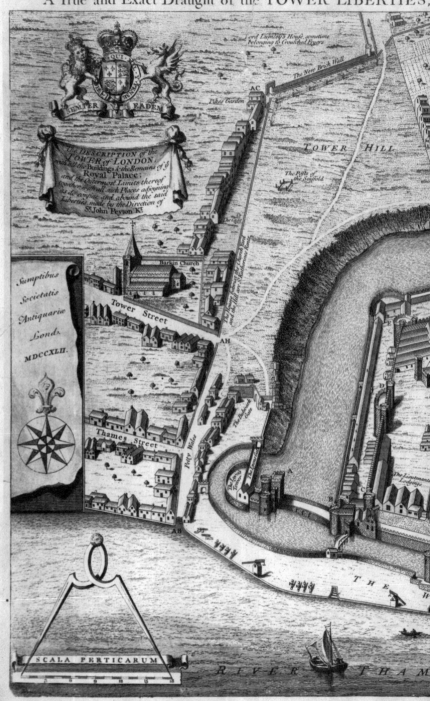